A PLACE BETWEEN THE TIDES

HARRY THURSTON

A PLACE

between

THE TIDES

A *Naturalist's*

REFLECTIONS ON THE SALT MARSH

GREYSTONE BOOKS

Douglas & McIntyre Publishing Group

Vancouver/Toronto/Berkeley

Greystone Books
A division of Douglas & McIntyre Ltd.
2323 Quebec Street, Suite 201
Vancouver, British Columbia
Canada V5T 4S7

National Library of Canada Cataloguing in Publication Data
Thurston, Harry, 1950–
A place between the tides : a naturalist's reflections
on the salt marsh / Harry Thurston.

ISBN 1-55365-035-2

1. Salt marsh ecology—Nova Scotia—Tidnish River Region.
2. Thurston, Harry, 1950– —Childhood and youth. I. Title.
QH106.2.N68T48 2004   577.69'09716'11   C2004-900271-6

Library of Congress information is available.

Editing by Nancy Flight
Cover photograph by Bryn Colton / Getty Images
Cover design by Jessica Sullivan
Text design and typesetting by Jessica Sullivan
Printed and bound in Canada by Friesens
Printed on acid-free paper
Distributed in the U.S. by Publishers Group West

We gratefully acknowledge the financial support
of the Canada Council for the Arts, the British Columbia Arts Council,
and the Government of Canada through the Book Publishing Industry
Development Program (BPIDP) for our publishing activities.

Every effort has been made to trace accurate ownership
of copyright text used in this book. Errors or omissions will be corrected
in subsequent editions, provided notification is sent to the publisher.

For my parents,
Betty Surette and Kenneth Thurston (1911–1974),
my first guides to Nature, with love

In this electronic age our perception
seems to be spread thin, diffused, as if our
environment were viewed from outer space via
satellite—so we get a remote view of life
on the Earth as isolated patches of light. We may
deduce that the rainforests of Brazil are burning
as a result of human activity, or that Indonesia, too,
is in flames from the effects of El Niño. This
information is transmitted to us instantly; we get
the big picture on demand. But how many
of us train our vision, and our ears, noses—our
senses—on the near-at-hand? How many know
what's going on in our own backyards, over time?
That is what I am striving to do, to create an
up-close and continuous record of a single place.
This has always been the naturalist's job.

AUTHOR'S JOURNAL, MARCH 30, 1998

CONTENTS

Acknowledgments   *xi*

Introduction: The Old Marsh   *1*

[1]   *January:* Red-tailed Hawk at Dawn   *9*

[2]   *February:* Tracks in the Snow   *29*

[3]   *March:* The Day the Ice Goes Out   *47*

[4]   *April:* The Rite of Return   *68*

[5]   *May:* A Rush to Life   *87*

[6]   *June:* A Tidal Clock   *108*

[7]   *July:* The Hidden Marsh   *128*

[8]   *August:* Twin Realms   *149*

[9]   *September:* A Time of Turmoil   *167*

[10]   *October:* The Sacred Hunt   *186*

[11]   *November:* Out of Place   *203*

[12]   *December:* The Boy at the Window   *220*

Notes   *233*

ACKNOWLEDGMENTS

I WANT TO THANK my mother, Betty Surette, and my two brothers, Gary Thurston and Greg Cook, for sharing their memories and correcting my own when they were faulty. I am indebted to the late Sherman Davidson for his observations and working knowledge of the Old Marsh. I thank our neighbors, Charles and Doris Bugley, with whom we share our daily delight in the Old Marsh. Thanks, also, to Bill and Sylvia Fairbanks for being our guides to the floral riches of the salt marsh.

I am indebted to Fred Hatfield, editor of *The Yarmouth Vanguard,* for sharing his story, "Man comes forward to say he knows what happened to missing boy" (Vol. 29, No. 41, February 24, 1995). Also, thanks to the Amherst Township Historical Society and the Mount Allison University Archives for aiding my research into the history of Tidnish Bridge and the Chignecto Ship Railway, respectively. Of particular importance was "History of Tidnish Bridge" by Pearl Atkins.

Special thanks are owed to my editor, Nancy Flight, for her steady and inspired guidance as the writing ebbed and flowed, and to my publisher, Rob Sanders, for his patient faith in this project. And, not least, to my agent, Dean Cooke.

As always, I am ever grateful for the love and support of Cathy and Meg.

Introduction

THE OLD MARSH

Y MOTHER, who is ninety pounds soaking wet, lifts me in her arms. I know that I had not yet been to school, but I cannot remember how old I was. Perhaps three.

She lifts me so that I can look out the bank of windows that forms a large dormer at the front of our farmhouse. The house is nearly two centuries old, and though still sturdy, even imposing, it is a bit down on its luck. It is weathered gray; whatever color that once adorned its split shingles has long ago been sloughed off like an outgrown snake skin. It sits on a hill and has a very high pitch to the roof, the builder having miscalculated when he built the trusses. The roof line can accommodate a dormer with three double windows, which yields a generous view of the salt marsh.

My mother wants me to see the moonlight on the river. The river is tidal and in flood. Spring tides. There is no snow, so I'm guessing it was November or possibly March. The river has breached its banks and spread far and wide across the salt marsh. Points of land have disappeared with this inundation. Only the high ground where black spruce trees grow appears above water as dark-mantled islands. Everything else is silver from the moonlight flooding the water.

"See," my mother might have said, "the moonlight. Isn't that beautiful?"

But something else in the water has caught my attention. There is a flock of birds floating in the creek near our swimming hole. I know they are ducks. Perhaps I even know they are black ducks. Someone has already identified them for me—my father or one of my two older brothers—and I now recognize them, their fat, dark forms, for what they are.

"Ducks," I say pointing.

"Where?" my mother says. Then she sees them, too. "Yes, ducks!"

ALL MEMORIES are a conflation but especially early ones. When I was old enough, with some effort, I could climb up on top of the blanket drawers built into the dormer, using them as a ladder, and look at the moon on the river for myself. Before then, my tiny mother held me in her arms. That memory is like a silver-tinted photograph, not because it is old but because it *is* silver—with moonlight. But there are also those dark ducks in the lower right-hand corner of the memory. When I first noticed them, I was surprised to see them there. But then, when I thought about it more, I realized that from my earliest days I was always looking for something alive in nature, something to animate the scene. I was not interested in still life. I was awaiting movement: a flicker of a wing, a darting underwater, a deer in the back field ready to bolt.

I grew up at the southwestern tip of Nova Scotia, a peninsular province that projects from the North American continent like a lobster claw. My home in pie-shaped Yarmouth County was situated where the Atlantic Ocean rounds the tip of Nova Scotia and merges with the Bay of Fundy. Properly, we faced the Gulf of Maine, across which radio signals freely flowed to our aquamarine plastic radio. It was always propped on a windowsill above the kitchen sink with a damp dishrag draped over it, which somehow improved the reception. Boston Red Sox games leapt across the gulf during the days of the erratic Jimmy Piersall and the splendid Ted Williams. What defined our place, however, was the Chebogue River (Chebogue is Mi'kmaq for "great still water"), which twice daily swelled with tide, nourishing the great salt marshes bordering it. These were and remain today the largest intact salt marshes in Atlantic Canada.

My home was known as Brook Farm for the small stream that formed one border of my father's property. Writer and back-to-the-land pioneer Scott Nearing would have called it a saltwater farm, as it fronted on a salt marsh like so many small farms up and down the eastern seaboard. Our market garden was planted in the rich marshland soil, just beyond the reach of the Fundy tides and salt. Above the marsh on a hill stood the house, and behind it barns, pasture, and woodlot, 40 hectares (100 acres) more or less, which for a brief time furnished an adequate income.

We lived both on the land by farming and off the land by hunting and gathering. Wild, or country, food not only provided a change of diet but was an integral part of our economy. We boxed wild blueberries and cultivated strawberries, shipping them on the "Boston boat" that ran between Yarmouth and Bar

Harbor, Maine; cranberries for sauce came from the bog near the gravel pit; blackberries for jams and jellies grew in abundance along a stone wall dividing the back pasture from the hay fields; and wild strawberries flourished wherever the fields were neither grazed nor cropped. My brothers and I picked these fruits of the Earth for my mother to process. They also gathered knotted wrack that grew in the muds at the mouth of the muskrat creek, selling this filamentous salt marsh algae by the burlap bagful to a local buyer who packed shad worms in it for shipment to saltwater sportsfishers in Boston. If he could, Dad killed a deer each fall; he and my brothers hunted black ducks and teal on the marsh and snared rabbits in the woods, and we trapped muskrat and mink on the marsh for cash. Each April, as a rite of spring, we netted smelts entering the brook to spawn.

We sold cream from the herd of a half dozen or so cows. My mother separated the cream from the raw milk, cranking the little black separator that sat in the porch, where the sweet buttermilk smell lingered among the coats and overalls hung there. Putting some cream aside, she churned it into butter for our table. In the afternoons, she baked double loaves of bread and listened apprehensively to the Bambino-cursed Red Sox. In summer, if the tide was right, she took me with her to the creek, where she swam in the sun-warmed water swathed in hip-high cord grasses.

Later, I also tagged along with my brothers, four and eight years older than me, to check our muskrat traps along the muddy banks of a branch of the creek. Soon I was allowed to visit the marsh alone. I went with a warning, however, about the hidden dangers: sinkholes, my mother said, could swallow me up.

Despite its dangers, the marsh became my playground and also my laboratory for learning firsthand about the cyclical workings of nature. It was among the salt grasses, which rasped my bare feet like a calf's tongue, that my love of living things—the inborn predilection for which Harvard biologist Edward O. Wilson coined the term "biophilia"—first came to fruition.

Most often I would meander down the path by the market garden to the mouth of the brook. Here, fresh water from a spring-fed wetland at the back of the farm mingled with the incoming tide and its salt waters. This was the meeting place for Earth's two great biomes: the land and the sea. It is this handshake, this biological reciprocity, that accounts for the richness of salt marshes, which are among the most productive habitats on the planet. Salt marshes are at one hour land, and at another, sea, depending upon the height of the tide that ultimately defines their boundaries and character.

THE SOUND I MOST identify with my childhood is that of the willet, one of the few birds that nest on the salt marsh. These brassy shorebirds were my summertime companions. Whenever I ventured too close to their well-concealed ground nests, they circled, dived, and incessantly scolded me as I played out my summer days. Although they meant to drive me away, to the boy I was, theirs was a welcoming call, a sign of belonging.

Events, however, were conspiring to exile me from my Edenic world of birds and fishes, and of aquatic mammals who very much like us survived by their wiles on that shifting ground between land and sea—events that a boy could neither apprehend nor control.

During the war my father had a ready market for all the cream he could produce, which was churned into butter for British consumers and the Allied war effort. But when the war ended, so did the demand for his butter. By the time I was school age, in the mid-1950s, he was farming part-time, milking the cows morning and night, before and after plying his carpenter's trade all day in town to make ends meet. The death blow to the farm was not dealt by faraway markets, however, but by the unwitting mistake of a neighbor. My father bought a milk cow, which unfortunately was suffering from Bang's disease, or bovine tuberculosis. The disease soon spread through the herd, causing calves to be stillborn or sickly. I remember ministering to one of these doomed calves with my mother. It was thin and wobbly legged, and its scruffy red-and-white coat was streaked with mustard-yellow diarrhea. It, too, died, and soon the whole herd had to be destroyed.

We hung on for another two years by selling gravel at two cents a tonne. Great trucks bodily carted off the farm to pave the road through the community. My parents soon faced a difficult choice. In the end they decided to sell the farm and move to my mother's childhood home in town. It allowed her to be closer to her dying mother, and they rationalized the move would in the long run be better for Dad's business as a contractor and for "the boys," my older brother Gary and me, as we entered our teen years. They were right on all counts, but at the time it was a wrenching experience. As my mother would often recall in later years, life had been good on the farm, for her and her children. Of me, she said I would leave in the morning and only show up again for lunch and supper. I spent much of my time alone, along the brook from its mouth to its headwaters, fishing for trout, catching smelts and eels with my bare hands, or playing at being the hunter or the hunted.

IT WAS THREE DECADES before I again called the salt marsh my home, once again could daily engage its sea-given gifts. In 1990 my wife, Cathy, and I bought a modern split-level house in the community of Tidnish Bridge, 20 kilometers (12 miles) from the shiretown of Amherst, Nova Scotia. Across the road lived longtime friends who had children the same age as our daughter. And in back of the house, a mere 23 meters (75 feet) away, flowed the tidal Tidnish River, named for the Mi'kmaq word "to paddle." Across the river was a 1½-hectare (4-acre) salt marsh, simply known as "The Old Marsh." It is a remnant of the 20,000-hectare (about 50,000-acre) Tantramar Marsh, a maritime prairie that forms the Isthmus of Chignecto (Mi'kmaq for "great marsh district"), connecting Nova Scotia to New Brunswick.

A hay barn had once stood there, a quarter century before, but all traces of it were now gone. A low dyke still surrounded the marsh, and directly across from the house was the remains of an *aboiteau,* or tide gate. It no longer held back the tides, however, so the marsh was returning to the sea, to salt marsh alternately covered and uncovered by the tides.

I realized that I, too, was returning to my original habitat. As we settled into our new home, I wrote: "The first day here a pair of willets flew over—*pitawee, wee-wee*—as if to welcome me back to the tidal river environment of my childhood."

I also recognized that the move was an opportunity not only to reconnect with some of the pleasures of my boyhood but to document them. I resolved to keep a marsh journal, noting the creatures that lived on and seasonally exploited the salt marsh. I set out to compile a phenology of the salt marsh.

ON THE OLD MARSH I was met by all the familiar creatures of my early, happy years: heron, willet, black duck, smelt, deer, and muskrat. And many that I had never encountered as a child: peregrine falcon, harbor seal, and hooded merganser, for example, and even minke whale. In a sense, these were the characters, stock and novel, in a new act of my life. Even those familiar to me I now saw with different eyes. Although my wonder and delight in other living things had not been dimmed by the years, my formal education as a biologist helped me to train a more analytical gaze on these characters that appeared in leading or supporting roles on the stage of the marsh. I now asked myself what drew them here and why at this particular time in their life cycle or in this season. What evolutionary adaptations had they made to survive in such a demanding, if ultimately rewarding, habitat? How did this community of living things interact—in other words, what was the ecology of a salt marsh? And I viewed this pageant of life being played out between the land and the sea—between the tides—with a more wary eye, one sharpened by my informal education as an environmentalist in the activist decades of the 1960s and '70s.

Like the dormer of my childhood farmhouse, my bank of study windows affords a wide view of the kidney-shaped salt marsh circumscribed by an oxbow bend in the meandering Tidnish River. To the degree possible, I have tried to understand the events and encounters that I witness daily from my privileged, albeit humanly biased, vantage. My perspective, at least from a physical standpoint, is very much what it was when my mother first lifted me up to the dormer in our old farmhouse. I see the beauty of the moon on the river, or a double rainbow arching over the greening marsh—an auspicious image that greeted us when we first looked at the house. But I also see the ducks, my senses always on alert for the thing that will give the scene meaning beyond its static and superficial attraction. In many ways I am still that boy in the window.

1

January

RED-TAILED HAWK AT DAWN

IT IS OUR FIRST winter here. After two weeks of brilliant holiday weather, day after day of blinding sunlight reflecting off blankets of snow and the mercury dipping to the bottom of the thermometer, it is raining. Through grim sheets of cold drizzle and the wraiths of mist rising from the river, I look out my study window and see two men on the ice. Curious, I walk upriver to check on what they are doing, expecting they are fishing for smelts. But they are fishing—or, more precisely, they are prospecting—for eels. With a chain saw and an axe, they cut holes through the ice at random and then probe with their long-handled tridents, hoping to strike an overwintering mass of eels coiled together on the muddy river bottom.

I had not thought about eels being in this environment, though it made sense that they should be. I was just beginning to learn about what creatures inhabited the Old Marsh and its river, who my wild neighbors were.

My neighbor Sherman owns the Old Marsh and has hayed and hunted there for most of his days. Like my father, he had once been a cream farmer and later went to town to work for a wage. He stayed on his farm, however, and is now in his seventies. Like me he keeps close watch on the marsh from his kitchen window. In a lifetime he has observed more of the marsh's drama than anyone in the community. If I want to know something about the life of the marsh before my time here, I ask him.

Ours is an ongoing dialogue between dedicated marsh watchers.

He calls: "Did you see that eagle soaring over MacIvor's? A great big fellow."

I rush outside, but "he" is nowhere to be seen.

When I first moved here, I often asked Sherman where to look. For example, where was the osprey's nest?

"In the cutting, on Irving's land."

Or the fox den?

"By the white birches, across from your place."

Sometimes he offered information. About bear tracks on the ship railway: "You could see the great big claw marks."

Or deer tracks. "The little fawn's prints," he said, pointing with his index and middle finger as if to punctuate the air with the forked prints like quotation marks around his story, "the fawn prints were following along between the mother's."

Sherman tells me that he and his father used to fish for eels, beginning in the fall and continuing into winter, when the river froze over and they would cut holes in the ice. They probed for eels with a six-tined steel fork. The middle tine, he says, had a barb on either side, the others only a barb on the outside. The fork was bound to a long-handled pole with fine copper wire. He probed the muddy bottom upriver, across from his house— not far from where the visiting eel fishers were. His father, he says, got more eels than him because he was more patient.

"I remember one day him and I were up there in the old scow . . . I hit an eel and it came to the top of the water and I threw the spear, and didn't I hit the damn thing dead on. We went over and got it. Well, he got the greatest kick out of that. He told that story to people more times. If I had told it they wouldn't have believed me."

I, TOO, WAS ONCE a fisher of eels.

Many summer days I spent on my knees at the mouth of the brook, carefully lifting water worn stones from their bed of fine gravels. I did so with the care of a sapper defusing a bomb. Under each stone I hoped to see the lithe form of a baby eel—an elver that would curl away with lightning speed, triggering me to grab a handful of gravel. I carefully clutched this potential prize, thrilled if I felt the eel struggling inside my closed fist. The trick was to nab the eel and hold fast its slippery form. Sometimes the tiny animal slithered free, wriggling to safety under another rock. Other times, I held firm, manipulating the mass of gravel until I could unceremoniously snap off the little eel's head with my thumbnail. Once it was dispatched, I laid out my catch along-side the others arrayed on a rock to dry in the summer sun. By day's end, the little eels, whose backbones had been visible be-neath their still-translucent skin, were brittle, crooked sticks, all color and vitality sucked from their commalike corpses.

Looking back, it seems a cruelly gratuitous pastime. I do not remember feeling guilt or remorse, however. In my imagina-tion, I was a fisherman like my grandfather and all Atlantic fishermen before him, dating to the sixteenth-century Basques who frequented our shores, processing their catch, using the sun to dry and preserve it. Only with hindsight could I apprehend the tragedy of the little eels, their epic journey from the Sargasso Sea, the mid-Atlantic spawning ground of all eels, cut short by my innocent hands after they had run the gauntlet of marine predators.

To survive winter, American eels—coiled in cold-blooded clots at the bottom of my river—depress their metabolic rate by as much as twofold as the temperature drops from 10° to 5°C (50° to 41°F). Rather than drawing on energy reserves stored as fat, as they do when fasting, they conserve energy by reducing demand. In response to lowering light levels and declining temperatures, other northern marine fishes either migrate to warmer (or deeper) waters or actually alter their blood chemistry. Northern fishes, like cod and smelt, produce antifreeze molecules, proteins composed of long chains of amino acids that depress the freezing point of their body fluids, conferring a thin margin of safety between surviving cold and becoming a fast-frozen block.

I am always amazed and humbled by the adaptations to stress made by so-called lower forms of life. Like the eels, many species have, through natural selection, acquired the ability to alter their metabolism. By contrast, we human beings have little control over our bodies. Our adaptability is principally from the neck up. Brain power has allowed us to devise technologies to counter the effects of changing environmental conditions (and to populate the Earth from pole to pole), but also, lamentably, to alter whole ecosystems to suit our needs, often at great cost to other creatures.

JANUARY IS LIKE A LITTLE ICE AGE, for a time weighing heavy on the marsh. For me, the marsh watcher, January is a kind of boreal blankness. Snowbanks against the tree line that borders the marsh, ice settles in the hollows, and the only emergent plants are the dry stalks of seaside goldenrod projecting from the top of the dyke and waving stiffly in the wind. This landscape will remain stubbornly unchanged for the next three months, except for the occasional breaching of a very high tide and the subtle shifting of snowdrifts, like sheets that have been ruffled by a restless sleeper. I scan this icebound world for animal life, often in vain. Crows, gulls, eagles, and foxes come and go intermittently, bringing brief drama to the often lifeless tableaux of the marsh. They are the lead winter players, but marsh creatures are hidden from my view under the scrim of snow and curtain of ice. What I see of winter life is only the tip of the proverbial iceberg. Although the visual signs of life are weak, I know a host of snow-and-ice-cocooned animals and plants are employing energy-efficient strategies to wait out the bitter weather. This paucity of life is an illusion.

Animals have three options for surviving winter's rigors: migration, hibernation, and resistance. The feathered migrants— the ducks, shorebirds, and other water birds—leave the feeding ground of the marsh and river for warmer climes.

Fish and invertebrates go into hiding. Fishes that winter in the estuary at the mouth of the river—smelt, tomcod, and winter flounder—swim under the ice; mummichogs and other salt marsh minnows have, with the onset of freezing temperatures, burrowed into the mud of the marsh pools, as have many marine worms and other invertebrates. Insects have laid their eggs in the tidal muds or in the ground above the tide or overwinter as pupae clinging to the marsh grasses and fringing marsh vegetation.

Many mammals—deer, bear, skunk, and raccoon—retreat into the deep woods or go underground. Muskrat periodically emerge from their bank burrows to graze on the roots of the

13

marsh grasses; the predatory mink, their nemesis, make night raids. Deer mice huddle together to keep warm under an insulating layer of snow. During the day they enter torpor, a resting state in which their body temperature plummets, heating up again for active feeding and foraging on the snow surface during the evening. Voles build tunnels through the snow; these seemingly aimless trails will only become visible in spring, transforming the lawn into an abstract patterning, like vermiculated wood.

Those animals that stay in place and are active in winter must resist—shivering to keep warm, scavenging for summer's leftovers, and hunting for the few animals, like themselves, that persist above ground despite the harrowing cold. For all such birds and mammals, winter, beginning with permanent ice cover in January, is hungry season. For me, too, it is a time of privation. My eyes hunger for some nourishment. Only the hardiest scavengers and predators cross my impoverished field of vision throughout the winter months.

ODDLY, I SEE RED-TAILED hawks more often in January than in any other month.

Part of our attraction to birds generally is that they sense the world around them much as we do. Unlike other mammals, for whom smell is the most important sense, we rely most on sight. Evolutionary biologists explain this fundamental difference by pointing out that our ancestors evolved in trees, where sight was critical to our ability to navigate from branch to branch. Even more so, birds see the world from above.

Hawks, in particular, have an extraordinary visual acuity, two to three times better than that of humans. Their eyes function like telescopes. Lens and retina are relatively far apart, the long focal distance producing large, fine-grained images.

Once considered rare in winter, red-tailed hawks are now relatively commonplace in Nova Scotia. Their numbers have rebounded since the 1940s, when federal regulations outlawed the shooting of birds of prey. Although red-tailed hawks were long considered a menace to poultry farmers, autopsies of these raptors—presumably ones that had been shot—exonerated them, showing that they overwhelmingly preferred small mammals (voles, shrews, and mice) to domestic and game birds.

Wherever its hunting territory is the rest of the year, the red-tailed hawk turns its gaze increasingly on the marsh with the onset of snow and ice. Deep-woods nesters, these hawks seek open ground for hunting, and in winter, when prey is scarce, they must expand their hunting territory, which is probably why I see them more often on the Old Marsh in January than in June. Day after day they follow a similar pattern. In the early morning, they reconnoiter the periphery of their ranges. During these so-called warm-up flights, they show little concerted hunting effort. These flights are usually short, a half kilometer (about a third of a mile) each, after which they return to a perch, where they might spend two to three hours. Heavy, relatively short-winged birds, they must expend a great deal of energy to fly, especially in winter, when they are not buoyed by rising air currents, or thermals. They prefer to hunt from perches, eyeing the landscape for a mouse or vole or an unsuspecting rabbit or bird.

The daily hunt for food in January's snowbound world must be achingly intense. For all top predators, this is true in any season. Energy is lost as heat from every level of the food web. By the time the solar energy captured by marsh grass reaches the topmost predator, the hawk, only one-thousandth of the original "green production" is available for the taking. My impression of hard times, however, is strengthened by the fact that the hawk seems to appear when bad weather is impending or during a storm.

On a bitterly cold day, which begins with a spectacular sun dog at dawn, portending bad weather, I spy the red-tailed hawk cruising over the tree line, where a raven briefly harasses him to no avail before reluctantly moving off. I am often stymied by the confusing silhouettes of soaring hawks, but there is little question when this well-named hawk cants so that I can see the upper side of the tail, as exquisite as an Oriental fan. The hawk continues to hover over the marsh, fanning its rufous tail feathers as it stalls in the frozen air, surveying the treeless terrain for small mammals.

The next day, I again see the hawk silhouetted at dawn, perched on one of the large poplars that border the neighboring marsh (Lucius's Marsh), upriver. In the scope I can see its breast feathers fluffed against the hard cold, an attempt to trap warm air and maintain body temperature. Despite the insulating properties of feathers, like humans, birds have little defense against the cold other than shivering, and even large birds must spend most of the winter shivering when not in flight.

Another storm day, I see the hawk sheltered in spruce trees, where he perches for hours as a wet snow blows in from the southwest—still and stoic, the very picture of resistance.

WHEN I WAS A CHILD, the boundary between the watcher and the watched was blurred. In the woods and on the marsh I was aware that animals were watching me as I was constantly on the lookout for them. I felt a kinship with the overflying blue heron or the deer poised in the back pasture. We were cohabiting sentient beings.

In *The Spell of the Sensuous: Perception and Language in a More-Than-Human World,* philosopher-magician David Abram contemplates the nature of perception. The sensing body, he maintains, is not some kind of "programmed machine but an active and open form, continually improvising its relation to things and to the world." That world, moreover, is in constant flux, the ground ever-shifting under us. One must be open to this per- petual dance of things. Our proper relation to the world, then, is one of reciprocity, of "a continuous dialogue" between the body and the things that surround it. Things, animate and inanimate, beckon to us, seeking our attention, even our participation. In this sense, says Abram, we are all animists. To those of us attuned to nature since childhood, such an active two-way conversation seems commonplace: it storms, I anticipate a hawk, and it appears. Such reciprocity, seemingly magical, is, of course, a consequence of long observation. I did not call the hawk into existence, like a rabbit out of a hat, but I did know what to expect from the shifting set of circumstances in my home territory.

In Native cultures, which historically depended upon wild animals (and plants) for survival, this reciprocity was encoded in their religious beliefs: animals offered themselves to the hunter, and without this gift of self-sacrifice, the hunter could not be successful. In return, the hunter had to treat all animals with respect or perish. Survival for both animal and human depended upon a reciprocal relationship, the brokering of a moral deal.

I experienced this belief system firsthand when I camped with the Cree of James Bay, where I had gone to write about their struggle against the Quebec government to prevent the damming of the Great Whale River in the early 1990s.

I lived with an extended family of Cree goose hunters for a week in early May, when the snow was still thigh deep. One morning I walked from the camp, consisting of handmade canvas tents sheltered in a copse of evergreen trees, to the coast. As

I was rummaging in my packsack for a camera, I heard a loud cracking sound, like a twig snapping underfoot or possibly ice breaking up. I looked up to see a herd of caribou, passing in single file 150 meters (500 feet) in front of me. (My first impression—I had never seen caribou in the wild before—was that they looked like compact, albino moose.) Surely they could see me, I thought. But seemingly unperturbed by my presence, they moved at a leisurely pace across the frozen creek, stopping at either side to paw at the beach straw and snow in search of lichen. The quiet of the landscape—the kind that seems to press insistently on your eardrums—and the pale, peaceful procession of the caribou cast an almost dreamlike spell. Then I again heard their anklebones snapping as they departed—the same sound that had first alerted me to their presence.

I returned to the camp buoyant with a feeling of privilege. My host, Robbie Niquanocappo, affirmed my feelings: "When things happen like that, especially up close and personal like that, the Elders say that the land has recognized you as a child, as its own child. It has recognized you as someone who is worthy of being shown these things. Some people like you come up here and never see anything. The land doesn't know them, the land doesn't want anything to do with them. In your case, there is probably something in you that the spirit of the land recognized. I know it sounds mystical, but that's what we believe."

SCAVENGING PLAYS as important a part as hunting for many of the animals and birds that stay to resist winter's onslaught of cold, wet, and relentless dark. Daily I am witness to their desperate efforts to acquire and conserve calories, which demonstrate a genius in capitalizing on the shifting nature of the marsh.

Large tides, generated at the full and new moons, breach the riverbanks and push through the derelict *aboiteau,* flooding the ice-laden marsh. Water also springs up through the ice cover, bubbling with the force of a burst water main. Crows station themselves at the *aboiteau,* jumping up and down in menacing crow hops, all the while keeping a cold eye on the amber waters as they rush in, bearing with them morsels of food, some random packet of protein and calories to ward off the winter chill. Sometimes the tide also releases prepackaged food like stickle-backs that had been fast frozen into the marsh ice.

Crows and ravens are ever vigilant and are among the most intelligent of birds. They are now recognized as having many of the same abilities, including tool use, as mammals. Over and over again, I see three crows working the marsh together—and on seeing them repeat to myself, "One crow sorrow, two crows joy, three crows a letter ... " It seems more than coincidence that I always see three together, and I cannot help but wonder if they are a family, living cooperatively, as we—my wife, my daughter, and I—do.

Crows occasionally do breed cooperatively with a yearling helper. This helper-at-the-nest is usually a mature nonbreeder who takes part in provisioning the young of the year. Such helpers delay their own breeding but may maximize their reproductive output in the long run by living longer, and in the meantime, according to the selfish-gene theory, they aid in perpetuating if not their own then the genes of siblings, similar to their own.

For my family, surviving winter is a psychological challenge only. Alone all day, with nothing but my own words and a window view to occupy and distract me, I anxiously await the sound of the bus bringing my daughter home after school, when we can sit for a few minutes and share a snack and the day's stories—which, for my part, often involves recounting what bird or animal crossed my vision. In later years, Meg will indulge her naturalist-father, asking, "What did you see on the marsh today, Dad?" In kind, I ask about the dramas of her human-centered affairs, of teachers and classmates, the nexus of her coming-of-age world. Meantime, my wife must battle the rut-riddled, snow-packed road through the Tyndal Woods to her work as a child psychologist in town, 20 kilometers (12 miles) away, leaving and arriving home in the dark. For most of three decades, we have happily reversed the traditional household roles; she goes to work as the main breadwinner, while I am the stay-at-home househusband and chief cook.

Looking back, I can see my choice of a solitary profession was seeded in childhood, when I was happy to spend long hours alone on the farm, exploring its diverse habitats, on the lookout for animals, birds, and fishes. Such a predilection, it seems, is in-born, though it was nurtured by the environmental richness around me and by the freedom I was granted by my mother to roam from the marshlands to the upland woodlot.

Economic survival in winter was precarious for my family when I was growing up. We dried off some cows in winter, so there was less income from the sale of cream. There were also fewer carpentry jobs for my father in winter, when outside work could no longer be undertaken. After the cattle were de-stroyed, there was no cream check at all. It was during this time that my father took a job away, on the South Shore of Nova Sco-tia. He was not paid, however, until the job was done, and as we awaited his return, our coal supply to fire the furnace ran out, leaving us with only the wood stove in the kitchen to heat the great ark of the farmhouse. Even with the central furnace run-ning, I could see my breath in the bedroom on winter nights.

My mother had grown up in a well-to-do home in town, but she had adapted to country life, cheerfully taking on many of the farming duties—picking, packing, and pickling produce from our market garden and tending the cattle, pigs, chickens, and geese in my father's absence. Without complaint, she had learned to be resourceful during lean times. My wife, the daughter of a doctor, showed a similar fortitude as I struggled through my early years of apprenticeship as a poet and freelance journalist, never once asking me to consider a change in career, even though it often meant going without the luxuries that she had become accustomed to growing up and that the modern two-income family enjoys.

Ingeniously, I now think, my mother stitched together makeshift sleeping bags from quilts and blankets. She, my brother Gary, and I slept in the upstairs hall, where heat from the wood stove would rise and stave off the cold. To me, at the time, it seemed like a great adventure, like camping out. My mother did not betray any distress at our circumstances, and I was as happy in my sleeping bag as in my regular bed—happier, in fact. Weeks later, my father returned home with enough cash for a load of coal and Christmas gifts under the tree.

A half century later, such a story might be interpreted as a tale of woe. But it did not feel that way at the time—in part, I suppose, because of my naïveté and my mother's courage. As I told her in later years, though we were cash poor, I had the illusion that we were rich, possessed as we were of 40 hectares (100 acres) of marshland, farmland, and woodland, each of which provided resources and recreation and a kind of freedom through daily contact with nature that has made me a country dweller most of my adult life.

A FAMILY OF RED FOXES lives across from our home. We call them the White Birch Foxes, as their den is located in the shade of two young white birch at the very edge of the marsh. Marshes and forest edges provide ideal hunting areas for foxes, which prey upon small mammals, nesting waterfowl, and insects in season. In winter, they pursue snowshoe hares in the bush and voles and mice in open country. On the marsh I often observe them scavenging.

In the wake of a storm, a fox circles the snow-mantled marsh, marking her territory along the dyke as she scours the ice and snow for food. She is the successor to White Face, the original vixen when we moved here. She is light-colored above, but not nearly so light as her mother, and bears strikingly dark leggings. I have given her the name Black Socks. Quick afoot, she sometimes breaks into a full gallop; constantly on the move, she seems to skitter along in a side-winding fashion, nose to the ground. She stops by the *aboiteau* to paw out a morsel, then continues downriver along the dyke, which has been breached this week by enormous tides. She stops to sample a large bit of carrion; I can see what appears to be a rib or perhaps only a feather sticking out of the snow. She does not linger long, however, finding the pickings—whatever they are—too spare. A raven, which has been keeping an eye on the fox's rambles, immediately shuffles over in comic sidesteps to finish the job, ever the opportunist, ever the vaudevillian in nature's burlesque.

This hunt for food is incessant, though moderating weather can bring a brief respite in the struggle for survival. January thaw is an expected and much anticipated event in Maritime Canada, when for a few days the temperature rises above freezing, temporarily loosening the stranglehold of winter, opening the land and water, and the eyes.

On such rare days, Black Socks lies atop her den, alternately dozing and looking about. With a detached insouciance, she lifts her head to watch the crows foraging on the marsh, as if holding court, surveying her domain. It is heartening to see her at rest, perhaps with a full belly for once. Her long, opulent tail curls around her like a comforter.

With the ice cover temporarily in retreat, a bald eagle drifts down the river, slowly, deliberately, covering the new leads of open water. It is fishing, probably for smelts, which winter in the estuary. When the ice is fast, as it usually is this time of year, the eagle repairs to the coast, where it scavenges for fish and crabs and other marine creatures washed up on the shores of the bay. I see it in the morning passing the marsh, stiff wings outstretched, throwing its great blue shadow on the snow, and returning again at night. Occasionally it perches on the marsh itself like a man hunched in a greatcoat against the bristling cold.

The brief warming that entices the vixen to doze in the open air and prises leads in the ice where the eagle might find fish is rudely cut short. The protean character of January soon reveals its harsher aspect. Freezing rain, then snow, sheets across the marsh, obscuring the ragged spars of black spruce that form the eastern horizon, sending the fox for cover and slamming shut any door to open water.

ALTHOUGH IT IS A COLD NIGHT, I have cranked open the study window to listen to the river's symphonic noisemaking: tintinnabulation, a booming of kettledrums, loud reports like the cannon shots that open Tchaikovsky's *1812 Overture,* followed by snare drum rolls as the ice gives way at a thousand pressure points and the river slides away to the sea at the moon's urging.

A band of mercurial moonlight on the river and marsh ice is exquisite this night, as I lean out the window into the crystalline air to better hear the river's percussion section beat and crash and roll, bringing a lively rhythm—moon music—to the play of darkness and light.

In the dark I must imagine what each sound means. A sudden crashing like a cymbal roughly struck—this, I think, is shell ice collapsing at the river edge or along the drainage canal of the marsh. In winter, ice is the most dynamic and musical element in my marsh environment. It is a stand-in for the dynamism of living things—for animal movement and bird song. I am sometimes appalled, however, at the seemingly senseless energy of the making and breaking of ice. Each day the river freezes, forming a finished if imperfect surface; then, as the tide drops, kicking away the ice's crutch, the river caves in. As it rests again at ebb tide, new ice forms, only to be broken when the tide again surges upriver, opening new fissures along the river's edge, which leaks a murky serum of brown, brackish waters.

What is the purpose of all this rampant energy? Exquisite ice crystals form, congeal into lattices both beautiful and strong, only to be split and transformed into slush or the fluid formlessness of water. Is this anything more than entropy—the sound of the universe grinding to a halt, driven by the still-mysterious force of Newtonian gravity, the crushing of matter into cosmically dense black holes? At times, this music of the spheres, this push and pull of the tides, offends me whose heart goes out to living things. In the depths of January I have to remind myself it is also the moon-induced tides, their repetitious cycles, that drive this animal- and plant-rich habitat.

It was also the movement of ice that created the marshes 10,000 years ago, when the Pleistocene came to a grinding halt. Of course, it did not happen overnight, although in geological terms the retreat of the Wisconsian Glacier was a relatively rapid event. Fourteen thousand years ago, all of Nova Scotia lay under 2 kilometers (about a mile) of ice. It is hard to imagine what kind of picture the landscape then presented unless you have traveled to Canada's High Arctic, as I did in the mid-1980s,

when I flew to Ellesmere Island, the most northerly of the Arctic islands, to visit a paleobotanist from the Smithsonian Insti-
tute who was studying the perfectly preserved remains of a
50-million-year-old tropical forest, where lemurs once swung
from limb to limb under the glare of the midnight sun. I strained
to take in the panoramic, breathlessly silent vista of the now
treeless landscape. In the distance were mountain peaks that
seemed to be swathed at their base in a thick swirl of mist. Re-
marking how beautiful it was, I was gently corrected: my host
informed me that what I was seeing was not mist but ice. Only
the tops of the mountains (*nunataks* in Inuit), some 2,000 meters (6,500 feet) high, were poking through the glacier. I realized then that the Pleistocene is not really over, that it has
merely paused. The ice is poised in its northern refuge ready at
the right climatic prompting—the periodic tipping of the
Earth's axis—to begin advancing southward once more.
Whether the present era, the Holocene, is an interglacial period
of prolonged ice-free conditions for the northern hemisphere or
a more short-lived interstade, a period of warming between
glaciations, even scientists cannot say for sure.

Not only was all of Nova Scotia covered with ice during the
last glaciation, but so was much of the continental shelf offshore
of the present landmass and much of the continent itself, in the
East extending across Atlantic Canada southward to Long Island
and northern Pennsylvania. Although the ice waxed and waned
with fluctuations in climate, for nearly 100,000 years it pressed
down on the continent with such force that it caused down-
warping of the earth's crust, depressing it as much as 75 meters
(250 feet) below present sea level. Then, 18,000 years ago, the
leading edge of the glacier began to retreat—mountains of ice
collapsed, giving up their great store of frozen water. As the
ice water poured into the ocean, sea level rose, in some places

60 meters (200 feet) above present levels, and remnants of these now high-and-dry, ancient beaches still rim the present-day coastline like rings on a bathtub. But as the glacial burden was lifted, the land itself rebounded, greatest where the ice had been thickest. Sea level dropped accordingly to a level close to what it was before glaciation. Today, sea level continues to rise, millimeters per year, as the land again subsides.

By 10,000 years ago, Nova Scotia was ice free, but the preglacial marshes of the north had been obliterated by the glacier's advance and retreat. Much of the sediment needed for marsh formation had been scraped away by the colossal blade of the glacier and piled inland as drumlins or moraines. New marshes were born again, however, in sheltered coves and estuaries where there was enough soft sediment and enough protection to allow the marsh grasses to root and expand. Such places are the mouth of the Chebogue River and the head of the Bay of Fundy, where I spent the first half of my life, and along the southern shore of the Gulf of St. Lawrence, where I now live.

In the northern hemisphere, people closely followed the retreat of the glacier, as the land rebounded and salt marsh— that fragile, fickle boundary between land and sea—emerged, a green ribbon clinging to the newly minted coastline. The oldest archeological site in eastern North America was discovered shortly after World War II, at a military base near the head of the Minas Basin in the Bay of Fundy. Carbon dating tells us that Paleo-Indians had camped there 10,600 years ago. They left behind over four thousand stone tools and several house or tent sites. They were hardy survivors: remnant ice caps probably still clung to the nearby hills, permafrost persisted, and the mean annual temperature hovered at the freezing point. These postglacial pioneers built houses framed by wood or perhaps bone, covered them thickly with hides, and stoked a central hearth to provide much-needed heat. The most remarkable of the artifacts uncovered were beautiful fluted spear points, fashioned from the multicolored chalcedony (agate) common in the area; they were finely worked and had prominent ears or "tangs" found nowhere else in North America. Attached to a shaft, they were probably used to bring down big game. The camp was strategically located near a migratory route for caribou, which in winter moved into the highlands, where strong winds swept the snow from the land, exposing the animals' lichen fodder. Probably these ancient peoples spent seven or eight months at this location. What they did the rest of the year is not known, but archeologists speculate they repaired to the coast, a few kilometers away, where they would have found a rich larder of marine resources—fish, seals, walrus, water birds, shellfish, and marsh greens. I like to think that these vanished peoples were the first marsh dwellers.

I PUT ANOTHER LOG in the wood stove in the basement and settle into an armchair, upstairs, to enjoy the light show of winter. On this January night, the moon rises directly in line with the river's course, a tremendous orange moon, a Japanese lantern. It becomes silver when fully risen; its reflection glazes the ice and seems to move upriver like a ghostly boat.

My wife and daughter are asleep, warm in their beds. I never feel more at ease than in these late, unharried hours, knowing my family is secure under one roof, and I am alone with a book, listening to the silence—interrupted only by the clocklike ticking of the house timbers as they contract in the cold and the occasional rumbling of ice in the river.

A loud call emanates from the woods across the marsh, a sound I don't recognize, neither a hoot nor a shriek nor a howl but very loud, consisting of four notes—more birdlike in its patterning than the call of an animal. A barred owl? Something out there is singing at the moon, mournfully, it seems, perhaps because of the harsh cold. The stars are out, stark and clear; the familiar Hunter with his belt and sword commands the night sky; and below, the Christmas lights still ring our snug houses.

2

TRACKS IN THE SNOW

B Y FEBRUARY, the marsh
ecosystem is locked down,
ice-fast. Open water is a
memory, and the river may even be smooth enough to skate on
for a few days. My fingertips freeze by the time I lace on my
daughter's and my own skates (my older brother's forty-year-
old, hand-me-down pair of CCMs, which I never grew into), and
we gingerly make our way, hand in hand, over the rubble of broken ice at the river's edge and onto the glassy surface, where any
tidal water freezes hard in an instant. A bitter northeast wind
propels us effortlessly. We raise our arms like crosstrees, transforming our parkas into makeshift sails, and fly upriver like cata-
marans, human iceboats cutting parallel lines into ice so clear
that we can see the menacing black waters beneath. Skating is as

close as one can get to flying when earthbound, just as sailing is on water. This day we combine both modes of pseudo-flying, racing upriver like hawks on our featherless wings and steel-shod feet.

Such conditions are fleeting and in most years do not occur at all. But in February, almost daily, I clamp on my cross-country skis, a venerable wooden pair with lignum vitae edges, and head for the trail that crosses the great Tantramar Marsh between my home on the Northumberland Strait and the Bay of Fundy. I ski at the end of a day of writing, but as the days advance toward the spring equinox, there is more light to prolong my excursions.

With the excitement of Christmas an echo now and the promise of spring still far off, cabin fever sets in. It becomes important simply to move, to vary the scene.

I am not the only one moving through and leaving my tracks in the winter woods. At the side of the trail, worrying their way in and out of underbrush warrens, are a confusion of snowshoe hare tracks: the long hind foot impression and the shorter front footprint like the period at the end of an exclamation mark.

Hares occupy a relatively small home range of several hectares and spend their days sheltered in areas called forms. They venture forth on trails or runways after sundown. The prime prey species of the boreal forest, hares live in constant danger. As boys we set copper wire traps in the runways of such "rabbit" warrens. The slipknot of the wire loop would tighten around the hare's neck, and in its panic to get free it would strangle itself instead. Never present to witness the fatal struggle, we thought little of it then. We were proud to contribute to the winter larder and relished the sweet taste of rabbit, browned with onions and carrots from our root cellar. I remember checking the snares set in the runways that branched off an overgrown woods road, which—if I'm correct—once led to the hardwood grove, long since harvested to fuel the kitchen stove. I do have a vague memory of the frisson of holding rabbits, frozen stiff, but whether these were rabbits we had snared, or ones shot by my father, I no longer know.

Few families are hungry enough, or sufficiently woods-wise, to follow this practice today. But the hare still has many wild predators—fox, bobcat, hawk, and owl—and in recent years a new hunter on the block: the eastern coyote. I often see its dog prints in the snow and its dry curlicue scat, rich in hare fur, and on cold winter nights I hear its plaintive cries.

In childhood I knew the coyote's call only from the sound-tracks of cowboy movies. It was a western animal never heard here until the 1980s when it made its final foray into eastern North America by crossing the Tantramar Marsh from New Brunswick into Nova Scotia, as well as into Maine. (Since then it has crossed the frozen Northumberland Strait to populate Prince Edward Island and apparently made it to western Newfoundland on drift ice.) The arrival of the coyote in the East was the culmination of a century-long migration and testament to the innate cleverness of this wild canine venerated in Great Plains Indian cosmology as the Trickster, or God's Dog. As is often the case with ecological change, it also had much to do with human activity. As humans systematically shot out the gray wolf, the coyote moved into its former competitor's range. Historically, the gray wolf was lord of the boreal northlands, while the coyote prospered in the arid grasslands and deserts of the midcontinent. But as wolves and big game were decimated, the populations of smaller mammals grew, yielding a constant food supply for coyotes—which steadily pushed north and east into the abandoned niche of the gray wolf.

I saw my first coyote in the mid-1980s, when a large wild dog, the color of straw, bounded across the road mere meters in front of me. It was an unnerving encounter. Although the coyote showed not the least interest in me, I was struck by the imposing size of this canine. The eastern coyote is conspicuously larger than its western counterpart, having, biologists believe, acquired wolf genes through interbreeding on its journey east.

Although we kept free-range chickens, this coyote and others in its pack never mounted a raid. The arrival of the coyote did create a stir in farming circles, however, especially among sheep farmers, whose flocks were targeted by this come-lately predator. Despite its long history of ineffectiveness elsewhere, a bounty system was instituted. Hunters shot coyotes on sight, fearing they would destroy deer populations. An upriver neighbor who had not fired a shot in a quarter century killed two coyotes, which, he said, had run down a deer on the ice and later returned to pick at the carcass. Such wolflike predators and competitors seem to trigger something atavistic in our nature.

Hunting in packs, coyotes will kill white-tailed deer when snow impedes this ungulate. The deer, too, is a relative newcomer to eastern Canada, having invaded this region in the late nineteenth century during warming conditions, which spelled doom for the cold-adapted native caribou population. But coyotes more often prefer easier-to-catch game, in particular, hares and rodents. They are, moreover, consummate omnivores; they will eat berries in season, insects, carrion, and even seaweed, which has sustained them on offshore islands. It is not only their catholic food tastes that have ensured their survival in a variety of habitats but also their nurturing behavior. Like all dogs, coyotes are highly social animals, hunting in packs for larger game and sharing food according to the hierarchy of the group—and singing in chorus.

I still find it odd to walk out on a star-bright winter's night and hear a pack of coyotes in full voice. It begins with a lone call, followed by a clear answer, but soon builds into a full chorale, an intermingling of voices and intents that are impossible to separate. It is not clear what prompts these chilling choruses: it could be a claim to territory, a warning to keep out to other nearby packs, or a wooing, an attempt to attract a mate. In February, mating season, the latter seems the most likely motive.

Coyotes are highly successful breeders. They are mostly monogamous, and the males fully participate in the rearing of the young by defending the den and bringing food to the entrance. These strategies boost survival rates of the three to seven pups that make up a litter and in part account for the durability and adaptability of coyote populations, despite concerted efforts to eliminate them.

DEER, TOO, USE the natural highway of the ski trail. Once I was literally stopped in my tracks as first one, then another, and another, and finally another, in quick succession, bounded across the trail, while I snowplowed to avoid a head-on collision. Perhaps they were being pursued, I mused when I had regained my composure. They had burst from the woods in full stride and cleared the 6-meter-wide (20-foot-wide) path in one magnificent arc. Like mythical reindeer, they seemed to fly, and I could only think they were escaping danger to warrant this kind of heroic action. Perhaps it was a coyote that flushed them from the sedentary safety of the deep-woods deer yards where they pass the winter months—but no predator appeared on their tail.

Most days on the trail are less eventful. But the relative peacefulness of the woods is its main attraction. When I stop to rest, it is the sound of my own heart, a muffled drumming, like the beating of a partridge's wings, that I hear first and loudest. Then I hear the chickadees, which keep up their charming chatter as they flit from branch to branch of the evergreens for a closer look at this upright creature with the ridiculously long feet.

In fall and winter, they form loose flocks of eight to a dozen individuals. Each flock follows a prescribed route, an invisible aerial path through the forest, traveling at the rate of about a half kilometer (a quarter mile) an hour and feeding along the way. The chickadees pluck a variety of insect life from under the tree bark—weevils, lice, sawflies, and spiders, as well as gleaning eggs, larvae, and pupae. The flock obeys a strict pecking order; each bird's rank is established by its aggressiveness toward a bird of lower status, which it chases and threatens. In February, the chasing becomes a courtship ritual between prospective mates. Pairs split off and follow each other, the female in the lead. The male feeds the female, a behavior called courtship feeding, in which the female crouches and shivers her wings, like a baby bird, when accepting the male's frequent offerings. Well-fed females have higher reproductive output, so the male has an interest in keeping her fat and healthy as a means of passing on his own genes. And when not feeding his mate, the male chickadee is kept busy fending off any intrusions by other males.

The trail travels through freshwater marsh—bogland—so it came as little surprise when one day I found myself following closely in the tracks of a moose. Not only were the great cloven tracks fresh, but this monarch of the bog had stopped to relieve himself and the impressive dungheap was still steaming as I arrived on the scene.

Moose are solitary creatures and are increasingly rare in Maritime Canada. The movement of white-tailed deer into more northerly territory has brought a plague upon moose populations here. The deer carries the meningeal worm (*Pare-*

laphostrongylus tenuis), which does little harm to the deer but attacks the moose's nervous system, causing paralysis and death.

I never caught up to my trailblazer, as he detoured into the frozen wastes of the bog, where I was loath to follow.

WHAT I HAVE BEEN CALLING the trail is the abandoned bed of the Chignecto Ship Railway, one of the grandest and most ill-conceived engineering projects of the late nineteenth century. It was the vision of one man, Henry Ketchum, a Fredericton-born engineer who predicted the ship railway would mark "a revolution in means of transport." He set out to build a railway over the Isthmus of Chignecto (the Tantramar Marsh), thus connecting the Gulf of St. Lawrence with the Bay of Fundy. His chief argument was that ships could thereby avoid the long and dangerous passage around Cape Breton and the Atlantic coast of Nova Scotia, bedeviled as it was, and is, by fogs, currents, shoals, islands, and reefs, not to mention the sandbar of Sable Island, which had more than earned its epithet as the Graveyard of the Atlantic, wrecking some five hundred ships since the late 1500s. Ketchum imagined vessels up to 1,000 tonnes loaded with western grain traveling from Chicago to the Gulf, then overland on his marine railway to the sheltered if turbulent waters of the Bay of Fundy, and finally to Saint John, Portland, Boston, and beyond. He spent the last twenty years of his life promoting his pioneering ship railway, which he considered far superior to the canal systems then much in vogue. He argued—interminably—that such a railway, capable of transporting steamers and sailing vessels, would open up the great market of the Boston States (New England) to the vast natural resources of the Gulf of St. Lawrence.

Ketchum secured the support of influential politicians and funding from British capitalists, and work began in 1887. Over the next few years he poured $3.5 million into his vision: massive masonry works were installed at the docks, heavy hydraulic lifting machinery was imported from England, and three-quarters of the double rail lines (the heaviest ever forged) were laid. Although the rail bed was perfectly straight and one-half was dead level—ideal conditions for building a railway—problems arose when the builders tried to ensure solid footing for it over notoriously boggy ground. In an area residents claimed was bottomless, engineers had to sink rock to a depth of 18 meters (60 feet) over 2 kilometers (1¼ miles) before bedrock was reached.

Although surmounting natural obstacles was costly, it seemed possible; financial disaster and politics eventually undermined the project. Disastrous deals in South America brought the financier, Bering Brothers, to its knees in 1890. The next year, Sir John A. MacDonald, Canada's first prime minister and a proponent of the project, died; and the following year Ketchum's company charter expired and was not renewed by Parliament. Ketchum never gave up on his plan, but his attempts to obtain further funding came to naught.

On September 8, 1896, he traveled by horse and carriage from his cottage in Tidnish (the neighboring community to Tidnish Bridge) to his townhouse in Amherst, some 25 kilometers (16 miles) away. Ketchum was described as "a fleshy man," reputedly weighing 127 kilograms (280 pounds), and it was a warm late-summer afternoon. Ketchum's health had been deteriorating for years, and later that day he died in his bed. The view of his friends was that the ship railway had killed him.

Ketchum's Folly—as it has come to be known—was a wonderful vision. Sometimes when skiing I imagine a three-masted schooner, iron-clad steamer, or paddlewheeler coming into view, seeming to float above the marsh on its dry voyage from gulf to bay. And I can't help thinking of poor Ketchum, always aware that I am treading not only on a man's dream but on his grave. Then, too, the ship railway seems to be another object lesson in the inevitable: Nature eventually reclaims even civilization's greatest works. Trees grow, insinuating their roots and branches into cracks and crevices, deconstructing the architecture. The birds and animals have reclaimed ancient palaces and temples and in the future will move through the ruins of our own steel and glass towers. For the naturalist, such an outcome is not a wholly melancholy prospect.

ON WINTER WEEKENDS, Cathy, Meg, and I ski along the ship railway, sometimes branching onto old logging roads, where, a generation ago, men and horses harvested the last of the old-growth forest. We have made such outings since Meg was a baby and I carried her, aboriginal-style, in a frame on my back. When she was old enough to ski by herself, we packed a thermos of hot chocolate to warm us along the way.

Once a year, my friends and I ski the ship railway from Amherst to Tidnish Bridge. We choose the first weekend in February to ensure that the lakes we detour across will be frozen. But for most of the day, we keep to the old rail bed, raised high and dry above the marshland and provided with 2-meter-wide (6½-foot-wide) culverts of quarried sandstone for drainage in the wetter areas.

We always cross Long Lake, the largest and longest of the series of marsh lakes, which include Round, Sand, Little Duck, and Big Duck. Long is a shallow lake that in late summer is half overgrown with wild rice, a silvery crop that feeds large flocks of wild ducks, though they no longer blacken the sky, as early settlers claimed. In winter, the ducks have moved on, but I have looked up to see a large raptor circling us. Unlike the other human marsh travelers—the ATV and snowmobile riders—we move silently through the raptor's winter world, with only the susurrus of our skis against the snow and ice, and the creaking of our bindings like the sound of a wooden ship hull cutting through the waves, betraying our passage.

The railway is lined for much of its length with mature white spruce, the first successional species, also known as pasture spruce for its reclamation of abandoned farm fields and cat spruce for its potent smell. Many are as old as the railway itself and have rotted to the core; every year some topple across the path. Other, more valuable species, such as black ash, once grew in this marshy habitat. So says my lawyer friend Bill, an expert amateur botanist who has co-published scientific papers on marsh flora, as we ski in tandem. Also called swamp ash, black ash was highly favored by Mi'kmaq basket makers, though now it is becoming exceedingly rare. The Mi'kmaq and their ancestors must also have traveled this interior hinterland to hunt moose and waterfowl in season.

The men and women with whom I ski do so to beat the winter blahs, to present themselves with a yearly challenge, and to keep fit, as I do—all motives that reflect our generation's luxury of choice. We pack a lunch and sometimes stop along the way to eat at a friend's camp left open in this backcountry. If people are home, we may be treated to a cup of hot tea and a chance to warm ourselves by a wood fire. We also arm ourselves with a friend's "moose juice," a freely mixed and notorious concoction of wine and pure alcohol. Although taxing, this annual trek is a lark, topped by a potluck supper and a liberal recounting of our mock heroics along the way.

In my father's time, people did not cross-country ski, at least not unless they had to. My father had an ancient pair of wooden skis with loops of coarse halter rope for bindings, stored in the garage rafters. Neither I nor my brothers ever saw him strap on these crude skis, which were fashioned from single slabs of hardwood planed to a barely tolerable thinness. However, my brother Gary remembers that when the road was blocked with snow—I have seen the old photos of people standing proudly akimbo on snowbanks beside the crosstrees of telephone poles—he strapped on an old catgut-strung pair of snowshoes and disappeared across the fields with a backpack to get groceries in town, 8 kilometers (5 miles) away. I'm sure he must also have snowshoed to the back woodlot to cut the winter's wood supply.

No woodland trail is new. Each is a palimpsest—blazed and erased, then retraced. Successive cultures pass through such wild lands, each for its own cultural reason, and before and after them, birds and other animals. Marshes have undergone historic reversals. Originally, the Tantramar Marsh was a vital migratory feeding station for geese and other waterfowl along the Atlantic flyway, especially in spring. The anglicized name derives from the French, *tintamarre,* meaning a great noise or din, which is what the waterfowl wings made as the migrants rose over the salt marshes. But those who heard this waterfowl explosion— the Acadians—dyked those same marshes, so many geese now overfly these once tidally nourished feeding grounds. In recent decades, dyke land is being allowed to return to the sea for the benefit of wildlife, society having decided the marsh has greater value in its natural state than as a hay and beef factory. By an accident and irony of history, the planned commercial route across the marshes—the ship railway—is now a recreational trail.

IN FEBRUARY I LOG fewer animals and birds than in any other month. The eagles, crows, and ravens, and my storm bird, the red-tailed hawk, make their rounds. Woodland birds—to

February

which, I confess, I pay scant attention the rest of the year—winter with us as well. Conspicuous among them are pine and evening grosbeaks. I recognize this finch clan at a distance by their roller-coaster, undulating flight—a crazy crisscrossing, a mobbing in the skies above the treetops. They dip and bob like aerial pugilists, coming to rest in the black spruce that grow to the edge of the marsh, there to feast upon a heavy cluster of russet cones.

The male pine grosbeak looks wine dipped, the female tinged in mustard. These colorful birds occupy the boreal forest north to the tree line and are more common in some winters than others. They are a furtive species, "irrupting," as the bird books say, into new territory opportunistically.

Their close cousins, the evening grosbeaks, are perennial winter residents, however. These "parrots of the north," with their great seed-cracking beaks (bone white in winter, pale green in other seasons), are frequent visitors to my feeder. These beautifully marked birds—yellow, black, and white— have a formal air about them, as if they were dressed for some important occasion. In fact, they are dressed for winter. Under the bold markings of their outer feathers, they possess a warm gray down to insulate them against the cold. Their feet are short so that they can tuck them under their plump bodies, and the unfeathered parts of their legs are covered with scales; the undersides of their feet have ridges (corns), which help them grip icy branches, inspiring one writer to quip, they are "equipped with snow tires."

They have become familiar denizens of winter backyards, but this was not always so, at least in eastern North America. Like the coyote, they were originally a western species that has made its way east in the past few generations.

There are other members of the finch clan, such as the common redpoll, that may show up at the winter feeder. An Arctic and subarctic breeder, this dainty bird with the jaunty raspberry cap is not found here in summer but in winter may be driven from its breeding grounds by deep snow or ice storms that bury its weed seed food supply. In 1855, a flock held Henry David Thoreau's fascination at Concord, Massachusetts:

> *These crimson aerial creatures have wings which would bear them quickly to the regions of summer, but here is all the summer they want. What a rich contrast! tropical colors, crimson breasts on cold white snow! Such etherealness, such delicacy in their forms, such ripeness in their colors, in this stern and barren season!*

Redpolls are considered erratic winter visitors, but there are winter vagrants who arrive other than by their own volition—unfortunates blown off course by the cyclonic storms so common in the North Atlantic in winter.

Not long after we moved here, in the wake of such a storm, I went to the local country store, which is not only the supplier of necessities and sundries but also the clearinghouse for news in this rural community. The store owner informed me that dovekies had been blown ashore, driven across the highway, and deposited in people's backyards by the latest nor'easter. Finding a dovekie in one's backyard is the biogeographical equivalent of looking out and seeing a flamingo knee-deep in the snow. These dumpy, black-and-white seabirds are the smallest of the auks (puffins, murres, and razorbills) and breed in Greenland and on other Arctic islands to the east. In winter, they gather in large "rafts" far offshore in the North Atlantic. Only a disastrous wind could wreck them onshore. Once blown inland, their situation is perilous, as their stubby wings and short legs do not allow them enough lift to take off from land. On water, like the other auks, they must taxi, beating the water furiously with their wings to attain flight. A biologist friend of mine found one of these wrecked birds struggling on the ground on the Tantramar Marsh. He took it home and, when it had stabilized, threw it from his deck into the air, whereupon it flew off, seeking the comfort of the flock and the wind-tossed Atlantic, to which it is so well adapted.

Vagrants and opportunistic species may come and go, depending upon the vagaries of weather and variations in annual food supply. But foxes, like us, are year-round residents, and I observe an upswing in their activity in February.

Some days there are only tracks to read.

This morning, hoarfrost covers the grasses exposed on the dyke top and a sea mist rises over the icebound river. On a clean sheet of snow is a single sinusoidal track, like a subatomic particle shot through the ether, a tracer, tracking where a fox crossed the river in front of the house in the night. With binoculars, I follow the line of paw prints, beginning on this side of the river, crossing over behind the dyke, then recrossing the river in front of the house, where they end abruptly at a lead in the ice, which opens and closes with each fluctuation in tide. It is a minimal narrative ending in a dark mystery.

But sometimes tracks in the snow tell a complete story.

When we lived in an Acadian-style farmhouse in the 1980s, one bitter but clear day I skied down the hill and across the pasture. Freshly fallen snow had hardened overnight, creating a clean sheet marked only by the parallel lines of my skis and, written over them, the blue calligraphy of shadow thrown by the bare limbs of the sugar maples and the beech trees. The parchment leaves of the beeches rustled in a slight breeze on the ridge above the field. Halfway across the intervale, I came across a second set of tracks and another shape impressed in the snow that told a story of the night before.

There, perfectly preserved, was the impression of the owl's body at impact, wings outstretched, tail fanned wide as it tried to slow its hard descent. I could clearly see the outline of each feather—in fact, of each barbule. At my feet was a mold of a deadly snow angel. The thin track of a field mouse, which had imprudently crossed the field under moonlight, was obliterated. Aesop might have made a moral of this meeting, but nature is no moralist. Hunger had brought these two—predator and prey— together. The Swedish poet Tomas Tranströmer has written: "The wild does not have words ... / Language, but no words." As with the owl and the mouse, the language of the wild is most often some expression—a rune—of the food chain.

ONE MORNING AT BREAKFAST, Cathy exclaims, "There's the fox."

The vixen pounces twice, coming off all four feet at once and landing on her front paws first. She digs a hole, perhaps burrowing after a vole or field mouse. Coming up empty, she urinates, pauses to stretch before moving along on her morning rounds.

"Yes," I say, "I saw her the other day near the den."

"She's getting ready," Cathy says. "It's a sign of spring."

It is a week later, after a brutal cold snap, before the vixen reappears. In fact, two foxes materialize. I presume they are vixen and dog, this year's potential parents. However, for the moment they seem to pay scant attention to each other, passing, it seems, without a sideways glance. Against the snow, like a sheet hung as backdrop at a rural Christmas concert, they seem intensely, almost theatrically, red.

The vixen—Black Socks—frequents her territory throughout February. Sometimes I see her crossing from the Old Marsh to Lucius's Marsh, upriver, but more often circumscribing the Old Marsh, following along the line of the dyke. Hers is a nervous energy, a skittish quickness, which I can only ascribe to her individual character—though, admittedly, all foxes are defined by quickness. She can be startled by nothing more than the wind or snow falling from the trees. She stops frequently to urinate, marking the Old Marsh as hers.

Foxes normally have a range of 4 to 8 square kilometers (1¼ to 3 square miles) around their dens and prefer forest edges for den sites. The White Birch Foxes have chosen the lookout of the marsh edge, just above the reach of the highest spring tides, for a home, and they have returned to this same den to raise their young for as long as we have been here—thirteen years now. On milder days, after her rounds, the vixen will bask atop the den, even in February's bitter cold. After snowstorms, she must do what we do—dig out. I watch as she paws the snow from the entrance closest to us. (As is often the case, there is a second entrance.) Foxes normally occupy an abandoned den, ready-made by a groundhog, and this may have been the case with the White Birch Foxes. But they have undertaken renovations; during our tenure, they have added the second entrance, which may also serve as an escape route.

We, too, have altered our original home so that we might enjoy the marsh and ignore the road and its civilizing effect. Mobility—in particular, movement at high speeds—seems to be both an obsession and a necessity of modern life. I've often thought that when archeologists unearth our civilization, they will be struck foremost by the blacktop tracks that crisscross the continent. When we moved here, our living room looked out to the ditch and the road. Although it is country custom to keep a close watch on what is happening in one's community, Cathy and I had little interest in the comings and goings of our neighbors (good neighbors that they are). We were accustomed to living at the end of a cul-de-sac, far from prying eyes, and really, it was the wild neighbors we were most intrigued by.

We decided to turn our back on the road and build a living room (which we call the River Room) onto the back of the house, facing the river and marsh. We designed it to maximize window space, at the same time installing a bank of windows in my study and a deck off the River Room. We turned the living room into a dining room and now use it rarely, except to entertain. Our focus shifted to the marsh, from morning until night, allowing us to spy on our fox neighbors.

Throughout most of the year, I see adult foxes singly. In February, the appearance of the second fox, the dog, stimulates new behavior in the vixen.

One night while walking the dog, I hear a strange hoarse cawing. I have heard this call before—inadequately transliterated as *ach, ach, ach*—under cover of night, and conclude it must be a crow or a raven, though I have never heard either make quite the same sound. Later that month, near the end of February, I am again walking the dog at dusk when I hear the sound, more like a bark, I now think, a yipping constrained by laryngitis. Then I see the fox, heading upriver, her luxuriant tail held straight out behind her. Black Socks pays no attention to us, trotting briskly along, all the while indulging in her strange introspective conversation. At first I think she is talking to herself, but then it strikes me that she is hailing another or at least advertising her presence, that it is fox mating season.

Not long after, I look out my study window to see the two foxes chasing each other, flicking along the marsh edge like grass fires. One ducks into the den, while the other stops briefly under the spruce boughs before disappearing into the woods. Courtship has begun in earnest. The pair, often monogamous, appears together again in the coming days. One follows the other, nosing the ground, assaying its prospective mate's readiness. Soon the two are rolling in the snow, tumbling over each other in a kind of roughhousing foreplay. Then they scrape along the ground on their bellies and sides, imitating and egging each other on, not unlike cats in heat. I do not see them copulate, but in a little less than two months I will see the fruition of this serious "fox-play"—when the first kits appear on the marsh in late April.

Besides the amorous attentions of the foxes, there are other promising signs of spring, as the Earth makes its annual orbit. The light lasts longer and grows more vibrant. It lingers at dusk, casting a reddish aura around the marsh. This rufous hue I call fox-light. It presages the flush of life soon to return to the marsh.

By the end of the month, the March sun, which announces itself as a sulfurous paling behind the black-green screen of the trees, streams so insistently through my study window I am uncomfortably hot. The cycle of freezing and thawing has begun to weaken the ice so I no longer think of trying to skate on the river, and the ski trail has turned slick with ice separating patches of bare ground. I crank open my study window, letting in the freshness of spring, like the smell of clean sheets on a clothesline cracking in the crisp air.

3

March

THE DAY THE ICE GOES OUT

Now that there is more light in the evenings, my neighbor Charles and I meet casually in our adjoining backyards after supper. Like most Maritimers, Charles is an inveterate weather watcher. "Baie Verte was black today," he says, casting a wary glance toward the glowering sky above the marsh. "You can always tell we're in for dirt when it's black like that." His augury of the landscape, born of a lifetime's accumulation of local knowledge, proves true. Winter blusters back with a vengeance in the following days. Snow and ice again blanket the marsh and the river, after a premature breakup in mid-March.

That breakup had been dramatic and telling of the perils of living on a river floodplain. It had begun overnight with twelve hours of torrential rain. By morning the river was in spate, higher than I had ever seen it before. Most of the dyke was underwater, and there was a strong flow through the marsh itself, a steel gray sheet of menacing force pushing toward the sea. The ice had broken into large pans under the pressure of the rising river, and I worried that they would jam, causing catastrophic flooding. The water was already well up on the lawn and continued to rise all morning, even though the tide was ebbing. I feared the wind would back into the northeast, holding the rising tide against the land. I called Sherman for his historical perspective.

"Oh yes, I've seen the river this high before," he said. "One time there was a river running right overtop the ice. This year, of course, there's been no frost, so the ice isn't hard against the shore. They say it's that El Neen-yo or whatever they call it, I don't know. But it has been a strange winter. It was warmer here than in Florida the other day.

"The temperature's going down, that's the good thing. The river won't come up with the temperature dropping. They say it's going down to minus eighteen tonight. Of course, I don't know, we have to take their word for it. That's the difference between us and them, I guess, Harry, they get paid for telling lies."

During the day, a bald eagle perched in a tree on Lucius's Marsh, across the road from Sherman's, like us, seemingly mesmerized by the river's rise. The marsh was now a lake, lapping the tree line. I was worried not only for our home but also for the foxes' den, as the icy waters were backed up against their front entry. Next door, the river was seeping into Charles's basement woodworking shop. At midnight, under a hazy full moon, I was still monitoring the rogue river. I had noted during the daylight that the river appeared only to flow one way, out to sea. The normal rhythm of the tide had been obscured by the great rush of fresh water. The incoming tide must have flowed invisibly under the layer of fresh water. As the weatherman said, it had turned bitterly cold. Outside, I could hear the ice—broken in a day—grinding and shifting ominously in the dark. By morning, however, as Sherman had predicted, the river had dropped with the dipping mercury and had backed off the lawn. The marsh was again frozen, and only patches of open water appeared in the river ice.

NO EVENT IS MORE keenly anticipated along the river than ice-out, and this is as true for wildlife as it is for us winter-bound river people. When that longed-for day will occur is anybody's guess and, I'm told, was once the source of a lottery in the community. In my experience it varies, depending upon the severity of the freeze-up, from early March until late April.

"Ice is an interesting subject for contemplation," Thoreau muses in *Walden*. It was of such interest to Thoreau that he kept record of when Walden Pond became completely open of ice each year:

> *In 1845 . . . on the 1st of April; in '46, the 25th of March; in '47, the 8th of April; in '51, the 28th of March; in '52, the 18th of April; in '53, the 23rd of March; in '54, about the 7th of April.*

For nearly three decades, between 1953 and 1981, Harry Adrian Davidson and his son Sherman kept a record of when the ice in the Tidnish River moved out to sea. They penciled the dates in large letters and numerals on the rough boards on the inside garage wall. The record begins in Harry's hand: "Mar 24, 1953 ice in river moving out." Thereafter, only the date appears, in two columns between studs. The first year they made a record is the earliest date for the ice going out. The ice also went out early in 1976, on March 26, and in 1979, on March 25. The latest the ice ever went out during these years was May 3, in 1967, followed by May 1, in 1961. Most dates fall in between these extremes, in April. The last date recorded is April 16, 1981.

This was no idle exercise, as it was important to predict the state of the ice in order to get the marsh hay from the barn on the Old Marsh across the river. The salt hay cut in September was stored there until March, when the supply of upland hay ran out. Then, at low tide, Sherman would hitch his workhorse to a sled and cross the river ice to retrieve a load of marsh hay. He says you had to make sure the horse had sharp shoes to give it friction on the ice, and when he returned across the river with a full load, he would stop at the gravel road to shovel snow over it so that the sled runners would not dig in and stick. "The cows really liked that stuff," he recalls. "They'd stretch their necks out seven feet to get at it."

I look for the first signs of the ice going out 3 kilometers (about 2 miles) upriver from my house at a bend known as the Wabash. This is the head of the tide, 7 kilometers (about 4 miles) from the coast, and open water occurs here first. Within a week the ice along the length of the river begins to rot under the longer hours of sunlight and, further weakened by the twice-daily tidal action, starts to move seaward in great rafts that batter and ram each other like warring navies.

It would be misleading, however, to give the impression that this transition to open water is a linear process; it is anything but. Spring in Maritime Canada is a painfully fickle season of brief promise and lengthy reversals, a meteorological two-step: one step forward, two steps back; two forward, one back.

Pack ice covers much of the Gulf of St. Lawrence in winter. This is the breeding and pupping platform for tens of thousands of gray and harp seals. Pupping begins in late February and continues until mid-March, but it occurs far offshore, near the Magdalen Islands and in the Northumberland Strait, and therefore out of sight. When I travel to the country store, to replenish our staples of bread, milk, eggs, and cheese, I keep an eye out for the state of the ice in Baie Verte, or Green Bay, so called for the fringe of rich salt marsh that transforms its border into a sea of green grasses in summer. Some days the bay is white, icebound: on others, black waters are visible, depending on the direction of the wind. Northeast winds—the storm winds of winter— push the ice onshore, while southwest winds—the predominant winds of summer—move the ice seaward. This seesaw movement of wind and ice may continue into late April, before the last pans dissolve into the warming waters of the strait and the gulf.

The tardy progress of spring relates directly to the slow warming of the waters. The sea heats up more slowly than the land, and its cold breath hovers over the region much longer than most of us would like.

Late-winter storms are common in March and may be dangerous for some marine creatures. Several years ago, following a late-winter snowstorm, a harbor seal—probably the young of the previous year—was found stranded by the side of the road in the Tyndal Woods, halfway between the Bay of Fundy and the Northumberland Strait. Had it originated in the bay or the strait? Either way, it was hopelessly lost and disoriented. Ice was still fast on the lakes and rivers, so it had crawled overland on its belly, some 10 to 20 kilometers (6 to 12 miles), seeking open water. I heard the story at the country store from John, one of a number of men who spend their free time there, trading local gossip and exchanging heated opinions about national and international affairs. He last saw the young seal waddling through the woods, turning downriver toward the sea. "No doubt," he declared with grim certainty, "it was a coyote's breakfast in a couple of hours." This harsh judgment of the young seal's fate might very well have been true, and for the coyote, at least, good news.

Hungry season, which begins with ice cover, continues through much of March. For several days at the beginning of the month—a time marked by thaws and the false promise of ice-out, followed by a nor'easter driving a heavy snowfall ashore—I watch as a fox returns to a cache of carrion on Lucius's Marsh. Ravens gather around, waiting out the fox, which occasionally interrupts its meal to chase them off. The fox returns daily to this cache, so curiosity finally gets the better of me. I pick my way gingerly along the frozen river edge and cross a small brook where the ice seems firmest. I break off a branch from a driftwood deadhead for a walking stick, knowing that a slip on the marsh ice could break my leg or at least soak me to the thigh. Circumnavigating the major creek dividing Lucius's Marsh, I arrive at the object of the mysterious activity to find a deer hide that had been stuffed inside a grain feed bag, perhaps by a poacher hoping to sink the evidence. It had floated up and grounded on the marsh, where hair tufts were scattered generously around the bag. Only the little fat clinging to the inside of the hide would provide nourishment, which indicated how important even such meager meals as this are to foxes and ravens as winter winds down.

Slim as the pickings are, they continue to attract attention from winter's scavengers. A bald eagle finds the hide, and I watch through the scope as it tears at it with its hooked bill, an instrument ideally suited to the task. It peels off strips of the rancid fat while holding the hide down with its talons. As usual, a couple of ravens taunt the eagle as they supervise its repast. When it flies off, they approach the carcass warily, hopping up and down. This, I believe, is a gestural questioning: Is this thing alive? If so, exercise caution; if not, tuck in—which they do. Ravens, cleverest of all of the birds!

Finally, in this parade of scavengers, a gray coyote emerges from the woods to examine the hide. It is the first of this elusive species that I have seen in a decade's marsh watching, and it proves predictably wary. Although no other animal is in sight, it approaches the hide haltingly. In the end, the urge to flee overcomes the attraction—it retreats upriver without tasting the much-frequented hide.

The drama surrounding the deer hide is not yet over. One day I look out to see the eagle again, as always, surrounded by a coven of harassing ravens, pulling at its tail feathers to distract it from its meal. This day the eagle's tormentors seem unusually emboldened and the eagle uncharacteristically awkward in repelling them. As it tries to rise from the ground, it suddenly tilts to one side, one wing up, the other down, nearly toppling in the process. With my scope I can now see what appears to be the problem—its talons are caught. In a reversal of the Prometheus myth, this great aerial creature is earthbound and subject to torment.

An eagle, even one in such a compromising position, is not a creature to trifle with. Its talons and beak and its great wings can do considerable damage, breaking a limb or ribs, gouging out an eye, ripping a hand. I must at least determine its situation and then call for help, if need be. I again make my way over the brook and around the creek, the traveling easier now that more ice has melted off the marsh. The ravens fly off as I approach, and the eagle redoubles its efforts to free itself. I can now see that one foot is caught in the mesh of the deer hide bag and that, alone, I am not going to be able to free it. I approach closer, however, to better size up the great bird's predicament. It regards me with a fiery eye and makes a fierce effort to fly away, at which the mesh suddenly gives way, and the eagle lifts off the marsh. Feeling the air under it again, it turns and flies upriver, in the direction of its winter roosting site.

AT TIMES THESE life-and-death dramas take on the character of a French farce; the comings and goings seem scripted for comedic effect.

Even in winter, foxes sometimes accumulate more food than they can eat immediately and create caches of the surplus. These caches are often found and exploited by other animals, including, I discover, other foxes.

Over a week in late March, I watch as a pair of foxes acts out escapades of caching and pilfering. White Face, identified by a particularly white brow, excavates a small hole in the snow near the den entrance and drops a large food item into this deep freeze. The next day she returns to check on the contents of the cache, tasting it before heading downriver. Not long after, I observe another, much darker fox making off with the cached animal—either a chicken or a hare, I can't tell. This fox also runs downriver before heading into the woods. Then, at suppertime, White Face returns, this time carrying a rat in her mouth, which she deposits in the cache.

Are these pilfering raids? It seems so; later in the week, I watch as the dark fox, much muddied from the rains, raids the food cache, making off with a muskrat stored there. A few minutes later, it returns and removes another partially thawed muskrat, which dangles limply from its mouth in a most unappetizing manner. The fox goes only 20 meters (22 yards) or so into the woods and returns yet a third time. Finding the larder bare, it disappears into the woods, but this time in the opposite direction from its newly created cache of ill-gotten gains.

What is this all about? Are these two animals really competitors, or are they mates with a different concept of housekeeping? It is yet another example of how our glimpses into the lives of wild animals are usually so brief and fragmented that it is often impossible to piece together a coherent plot of their lives and motivations, however vigilant we might be. We see what we can see—we observe their actions—but we cannot always intuit their meaning for the simple reason that we do not think, as the poet said, in the language of the wild, as foxes do.

ALTHOUGH MY NEIGHBORS and I may not be able to call the date the ice will leave the river, the birds know the instant there is open water. Common mergansers make a beeline upriver and appear at the Wabash seemingly the moment it opens. The belted kingfisher, that halcyon bird, materializes above a narrow patch of black water, dives like a circus daredevil into a bathtub-sized hole in the ice, and to my surprise comes up with a silvery fish twitching in its oversize beak. Other feathered and furred fishers will follow the lead as more of the river shakes off its icy mantle, until one day it is ice free. One morning I wake and blink in the familiar but seemingly fresh vista; the dark aqueous eye of the river stares back, its cataract of winter removed.

The biological implications of this event are profound. The light that all winter has been blocked by ice and snow cover floods into the water column, fueling the exponential growth of phytoplankton. This proliferation of microscopic plant life feeds a host of marine organisms—from the tiniest zooplankton, such as copepods, mysids, amphipods, and rotifers, to the larvae of larger marine organisms such as crabs, snails, clams, worms, and starfish. These small animals, in turn, feed larval fishes that develop in the nurseries of marsh creeks, estuaries, and shallow bays.

Dead plant material, so-called detritus, is perhaps the most important food source in the salt marsh ecosystem. The ice that has ridden up on the marsh, settling there for the winter, has sheared off the plant tops and, like natural grist stones, has ground the bases of the marsh grasses into meal. As the ice backs out to the sea, it takes with it some of this pulverized plant material, and what remains behind is flushed out by the large spring tides. It is fed upon by a hardy group of small organisms known as detritus eaters, bottom-dwelling invertebrates that are capable of digesting the coarse plant matter. If they cannot, bacteria and fungi break down the tough cellulose for them. The bottom dwellers then ingest the bacteria and fungi. One way or another, the great store of energy produced by the tidally nourished plants the year before is given back to the sea, where it is entrained and exchanged in a complex marine food web.

ICE-OUT RELEASES FOOD, sound, smell, and sight, enlivening the senses. Life quickens on the Old Marsh with the return of migrants, exiled for long months by the ice and snow.

Most are fishers of one kind or another. As the kingfisher demonstrates, minnows are emerging from their winter homes in the mud; in the estuary there is a mustering of schools of smelt, readying themselves for their spawning run into fresh water once the water reaches the optimum temperature. Winter flounder, which have bred in the inshore waters during the winter, are moving offshore, to be replaced by summer flounder migrating landward from the ocean depths, in a piscatorial changing of the guard.

The common mergansers fly ramrod straight, bill, head, body, and tail on the same horizontal axis, their wings seemingly rotating on this axis like those on a whirligig. Their flight appears programmed, as they follow the lifeline of the river precisely, unwavering in their sense of purpose. When I see a flock pass, it's as if I am watching a squadron perform a synchronized air show, without the hellish noise of jet engines thundering overhead. Male mergansers, with their iridescent green heads and white bodies, seem as crisply turned out as sailors. Handsome as they are, I await, impatiently, the return of their diminutive cousins, the hooded mergansers, which follow only, it seems, when the river has completely cleared of ice.

I look out one morning to see a pair at the *aboiteau*. The male is resplendent in his breeding plumage, his showy white crest raised like the helmet decoration of a Roman centurion or the headdress of an Aztec warrior. The female dives frequently, while the male, following behind, keeps its brilliant golden eyes on its prospective mate. When he turns broadside to the sun, his crest flashes like a beacon in the strong spring light. These strangely beautiful birds will stay only a few days before seeking an inland breeding ground, near a river or lake, where they will make a nest in the cavity of a large tree or woodpecker hole or occupy a nest box erected for wood ducks. For a short time, however, in early spring and again in the fall, I have the pleasure of their exotic company. They feed in the river and on the flooded marsh with great success, snagging sticklebacks, which they must maneuver with their sawtoothed bills from a crosswise position so that they can swallow the fish by the head, heavy end down. Often they drop their protesting prey, only to immediately catch it once more and again begin tossing and turning it. They swallow the fish whole, and I wonder whether they feel the prickly spines of the stickleback as it slides down their gullet.

"Fish ducks," my father would say whenever a merganser flew by, as we fished for trout in an inland stream. He disdained them for two reasons. Of course, they are fish eaters, and thus their flesh is "fishy," so he would caution his sons never to lose patience and shoot one. (My father was not alone in his negative opinion of the mergansers' culinary qualities. I remember being at a fish camp in the interior of the Ungava peninsula with the Cree when a mother burst from her cooking tent to admonish her sons, who were setting out in a canoe on a hunting expedition: "No more of *those* ducks!") Then, too, mergansers eat trout, which put them in direct competition with us. "Fish ducks," he would say, as if uttering a curse.

NOT ALL THE FISHERS are feathered; some are furbearers. March, "in like a lion," dumps 40 centimeters (16 inches) of snow on us, and as I look out at the white wastes of the marsh I see a medium-sized furbearer scramble under a driftwood log, seeking shelter from the storm. In a couple of hours, the log is drifted over with snow. Two days later, freezing rain and mist shroud the marsh when a mink pops up by the *aboiteau,* poking its head above the shore-fast ice. It is a large black animal with a prickly look to it—its oily guard hairs sticking out perpendicular to its body, glistening in the low light. It has a small fish clamped in its jaws, and at first the animal appears large enough to be an otter. It is, however, a mink—by its size surely a male—and I realize it is probably the clandestine visitor I saw earlier, burrowing under the log.

The mink's unexpected appearance releases a long-buried childhood memory. It is a story that I am reluctant to relate, as it seems so much like a tall tale in its unexpected outcome. There is, however, nothing fanciful about my memory of events. This is the way it happened.

Outbuildings faced the back of the farmhouse, a two-story garage and a woodshed, which were connected, and the outhouse, which stood separately. I often played in the woodshed, where we stored slab wood for the kitchen stove. It had a dirt floor, and one day—for reasons I cannot remember—I was sitting on my haunches and happened to look under the landing for the stairway that led up to the second story. Staring back at me was a pair of fierce feral eyes, glowing in the gloaming of the dark shed. I was startled and later confided to my mother that there was an animal living under the woodshed stairs.

I was an imaginative child (I invented whole baseball leagues and spent many days bouncing a red, white, and blue rubber ball off the high roof of the house, all the while announcing each play at the top of my lungs, to the distraction of my parents and more mature brothers). Perhaps my mother dismissed this animal as some phantom of playtime. I was also the youngest in the family, and therefore my opinion was often lightly regarded. I began to doubt the truth of what I had seen. But each time that I summoned the courage to look under the steps, there they were, those icy eyes, looking back.

Often my brother Gary and I would spend summer days with my father's parents in town. My grandmother sewed each of us a money bag from the kid leather she used to fashion gloves for the ladies of Yarmouth. With nickels and dimes jangling within, we lined up at the Capitol Theatre for the Saturday B-grade matinees—the Bowery Boys and the Three Stooges, Lone Ranger and Tarzan epics. My father would pick us up after he finished his six-day work week on Saturday afternoons. As much as I liked the movies, and as much as I loved my grandparents, I soon began to skip these regular trips to town. I preferred the playground of the farm to the streets and sandlots of Yarmouth.

It must have been during one of these weeks, when my brother was in town and I had stayed at home, that I first encountered the hypnotic eyes under the woodshed steps—otherwise I would have, by then, cajoled him into taking a look.

I stuck to my story, and finally, on a Sunday—the one day my father did not work off the farm—I convinced the family to follow me to the shed. Their motive may have been to prove me wrong and thus rid themselves of my pestering. As we made our way across the yard, I worried that the eyes would not be there, that my animal had disappeared overnight, or worse, that I *had* imagined it. But when my father got down on his knees to see for himself, he exclaimed, "Well, I'll be damned."

"What is it?" my mother said.

Dad didn't answer but looked around for a stick of slab wood.

"Be careful," Mom said.

Dad poked under the steps. Suddenly a mink shot out, sending everyone scurrying backward. Seeing us and the light from the shed door, he bolted for the light, leaping into the backyard.

The strong summer light seemed to daze the animal so long sequestered in the dark of the woodshed. It turned in confused circles before making a run for it. During this commotion, I did not see Gary take up the clothesline pole, fully twice as long as he was tall. But I did see him release it, like an Olympian immortalized on an ancient Greek vase. The pole arced and struck the streaking mink broadside, killing it instantly.

The chances of actually hitting the mink were minuscule, which is why the story seems so farfetched—even to me, who was there. Perhaps no one was more surprised than my brother. He proudly claimed the prize of the mink, which my father skinned and stretched. It sold for twenty dollars, a princely sum in those days. More important to me, I was vindicated: I had seen what I said I had seen.

What the mink was doing far from its marsh habitat, or water of any kind, hiding for days in the woodshed, no one knows. Gary recalls that the muskrat population had crashed about this time, probably partly because of predation by mink. A male mink—like the ones at the *aboiteau* and in the woodshed—is large enough to kill muskrats. Like most weasels, mink are formidable predators for their relatively small size. A semiaquatic animal with partially webbed feet and oily fur to insulate it from frigid northern waters, mink eat mostly fish; on land, however, they will hunt rodents, hares, frogs, snakes, and birds. In my imagination, they might also have hunted small boys.

FOR THE NATURALIST who puts down roots as I have, there are two distinct kinds of pleasures that derive from being in one place over time and tracking the rounds of the seasons. The first relates to the expected, the ability to predict what will happen at certain times of the year—when the spring and fall migrants will appear and disappear, when the fish will make their spawning runs, when the birds will begin nesting or the first fox kits emerge from their den by the white birches, or even when I might expect to see the first deer cropping marsh grass. Then there is the unexpected: the first and only time you might spy a rare species, or the infrequent visits from a little-seen animal or bird. It is difficult to choose between the two, the satisfaction of one being equal to the excitement of the other.

March seems to deliver both the comfort of the familiar and the exhilaration of surprise. One day at the end of March, I arrive home midday to see a great bull gray seal making its lugubrious way upriver, against the ebbing tide. It moves slowly, ponderously, sometimes arching its back to dive, but mostly sculling along with its head out of water, like a gentleman in a straw boater from an unhurried, bygone era. Such a great head—which has earned it the sobriquet "horse head," and its scientific name *Halichoerus grypus,* Latin for "hook-nosed pig of the sea." Spiky whiskers bristle its fleshy snout and shine in the sun like fiber optics, receiving bytes of sensory information I cannot begin to decipher. But it is by this prominent Roman nose, which is convex, rather than concave, that I can distinguish a gray seal from its smaller relative, the harbor seal. Also, its great size—up to 300 kilograms (660 pounds) for a male like this one—leaves little doubt of its identity. It has come in from the strait, where it has bred on the ice, probably lured inland by fish moving upriver from the estuary. Or perhaps it is merely exploring—its manner seems so casual. At the bend above our house, where the river elbows, it treads water, then sinks, its telltale head slowly submerging. To the impressionable, such an outsize, even monstrous, head might inspire stories of Nessie and the like.

Other aquatic furbearers make their appearance before March is out, now that the river highway is again open.

The phone rings; it's Charles: "Did you see that otter? He's just below us, he's eating some kind of fish."

"I'll take a look and give you a call back." I run into the living room to have a look through the scope. The otter—the first one I've seen since moving here—has come up in a lead in the ice and is trying to finish off the head of the fish. It looks like a salmon head, being too big, I think, even for one of the sea trout that run upriver in spring. I doubt my diagnosis, as there are very few Atlantic salmon left in the river since its spawning grounds have become laden with silt as a result of clear-cutting in the headwaters. Whatever it is eating, I am impressed by the mechanics of the otter's teeth; its great molars seem to crush the fish head with the same ease with which I eat an apple.

I call Charles back: "I don't know what it was eating. It looked like a salmon, but then it might have only been a big sucker. I couldn't see it clearly enough. It's great to see them, eh?"

"I know. Years ago, Sherman used to trap them upriver," Charles says. "I hadn't seen otters down here before."

THE INCREASED ACTIVITY of late March is not confined to the water but surges onto the land and into the air.

Two hunchbacked forms skulking across Lucius's Marsh prove to be raccoons. With the ice gone, they have ventured onto the marsh in broad daylight to see what winter leftovers they might scavenge. How devious they look, even at a distance, as if they were up to no good. It is not only their masks—and their audaciousness—that give them their reputation as bandits, but I now see it is their posture, too. They are hunched, as if they are hiding their heads under turned-up collars, like suspicious characters on a shady street. Skunks, too, have come out of semihibernation; later, when the frost is gone, they will drill my lawn at night for grubs, leaving their telltale holes. Now, it is only their scent that lingers in the night air. It is like the smell of the marsh itself, pungent, mephitic, as marsh gases bubble to the surface with the warming temperatures. Skunk smell is a heartening odor; it announces spring and wakens the somnolent senses like a blast of smelling salts. For me it is also a nostalgic smell. I remember how welcome that commingling of odors from the marsh and iodine from the sea was when I crossed the Tantramar Marsh into Nova Scotia after a two-year absence in Central Canada. Smelling it, I knew I was home; smelling skunk, I know it is spring at last.

Land birds are also returning—robins and grackles in the vanguard—probing the lawn for food but also working the newly exposed marsh. And my family of crows is doing its spring cleaning on the marsh, carrying out its yeoman environmental function. I compare crows to the bottle pickers that appear along Maritime roads this time of year. We pass them with a sense of pity, that they must pick bottles from the ditch for pennies, but we should praise them for this seasonal work that keeps us from drowning in an accumulation of our own careless acts.

We have all heard the old saw "Nature abhors a vacuum," and year after year I observe practical demonstrations of this principle that apply to the marsh habitat. Open river, mergansers. Open marsh, harrier. Open marsh pools, black ducks. A day doesn't pass between the availability of a niche and the arrival of its rightful exploiter.

The skies, too, are opening, though you might argue they are always so. Warmer air rising from the land provides a new ladder for soaring birds, primary among them the resident bald eagles. All winter, eagles have passed by on their excursions from their upriver roosting sites to the coast and back again in the evening, occasionally stopping by to perch atop a black spruce, their piebald heads occulting like lighthouse lanterns as they scan the landscape, or to hunch on the marsh, Atlas-like, seeming to shoulder the sky itself. Now, as the late-March sun sends up thermals, the eagles circle the marsh in ever-mounting spirals.

Now, too, I see them not only singly, enjoying their powers of flight, but soaring together, a courtship behavior that helps to renew their bonds—which may be lifelong. Sometimes the breeding birds will lock talons and cartwheel toward the earth.

Growing up in the 1950s, I cannot remember seeing bald eagles at all, even though the Chebogue River was potentially suitable habitat, especially in winter when the river remained ice free. As top predators, eagles are necessarily less numerous than prey species, but to explain their near absence in eastern North America during my childhood we must look for other reasons. Until the middle of the twentieth century, eagles were hunted and killed with impunity, largely because they were seen as threatening to domestic and game animals. In the face of drastically reduced populations, both Canada and the United States passed laws for protection of raptors—eagles and hawks—in the 1950s and 1960s. By then, however, another, more insidious agent was decimating populations: organochlorine compounds such as DDT and dieldren. These insecticides, derivatives of nerve gases developed during World War II, accumulated in fat tissues of organisms, and their effect became magnified as they rose through the food chain, causing eggshell thinning in raptor species and poor survival of any young that did manage to hatch. The use of these substances threatened to empty the skies, rivers, the Earth itself, of many valuable species, not least among them, salmon, peregrine falcons, and eagles.

DDT was banned in both Canada and the United States in the 1970s, and since that time eagle populations have rebounded dramatically, especially in eastern Canada. In 1975 there were an estimated sixty-five eagle pairs in Nova Scotia; today there are at least two hundred. The largest numbers are centered on the brackish Bras d'Or Lake, an inland sea on Cape Breton Island. But nearly every suitable river on the mainland now has at least one eagle pair. I am convinced that there are at least three pairs nesting on the Tidnish River, having seen six adults soaring majestically over the marsh at one time.

Eagles usually nest near water in the topmost branches of the highest tree to provide a view over the surrounding canopy. They begin laying in mid-March, usually two, sometimes three, eggs. Male and female take turns incubating the eggs for thirty-five days. If food is scarce, the youngest bird is allowed to die or may be devoured by its siblings. The male provisions the nest with an eclectic diet of fish, waterbirds, rodents, and hares while the female shreds the prey or carrion for easy feeding to the eaglets. In twelve weeks, the survivors will take to wing, distinguishable from their parents by a lack of white feathering on head and tail, which takes four years to fully develop.

I see immature eagles almost as frequently as mature ones, assuring me that the population is being replaced, that the poisonous rain of insecticides that fell during my childhood years has largely worked its way out of the system.

TWICE EVERY MONTH the tides are especially high. We call them spring tides, from the Anglo-Saxon word *springen,* "to leap up." These high tides occur at the full and the new moons, when the sun and the moon are in alignment with the Earth and therefore, together, exert greater gravitational pull on the ocean's waters. The spring tides tend to be especially high in the spring and the fall, during the equinoxes, because of the declination of the moon and the sun with respect to the Earth's equator. The factors influencing tides—some two hundred of them—can amplify or minimize tidal range, but suffice it to say that March is often a time of unusually high tides. These particular spring tides have an important function in opening up the ecosystem.

The highest tides entirely flood the marsh, bursting through the derelict *aboiteau,* until only the top of the dyke pokes above the sepia-colored waters like a battlement. When one of these spring tides recedes, I can see, for the first time in months, islands of bare marsh. With each succeeding spring tide, these islands grow in size and coalesce until nearly the whole marsh is ice free. The brittle, brown stalks of seaside goldenrod wave in the wind, a harrier flies low on its stiff wings over its newly exposed hunting ground, and a killdeer's harsh call rings out.

Sound, other than the mechanics of ice, again begins to define my world. It is not only as if bandages have been taken from my eyes but also as if cotton has been removed from my ears. Still, the senses seem rusty, out of practice, somehow. So it takes me a few seconds to connect a faintly familiar sound to its maker. The clangor sounds like old ox bells echoing in a distant field. Then the auditory memory directs my eyes upward, where I see a flock of geese—perhaps a hundred strong—wedging their way north.

Their calls are the most potent sign of imminent spring for us northerners, and their arrival is intimately related to the clearing of the ice from the marsh. While the uplands may still be covered with snow and ice, the salt marsh is cleared early by the high spring tides. Moving north cautiously, egged on by southerly winds and forced to retreat by northerlies—two steps forward, one back—the geese converge on these ice-free marshes to feed. They strip what vegetation the ice has left standing, excavate for roots, and glean what little new growth has begun to push its way toward the sun. When food is available nowhere else, it is there for the taking on the marsh and critical to the geese's successful migration north to the breeding grounds.

With the ice gone for good, spring leapfrogs forward. The marsh poises for a greening that will support a legion of new life. As Thoreau said, the breaking up of ice from rivers and ponds "is particularly interesting to us who live in a climate of so great extremes." To northern marsh dwellers like me, there is no more exhilarating event in the round of seasons than the day the ice goes out. It promises the return of the many migrants and marsh breeders that give meaning to my days, engaging my senses, allaying my solitude. One by one the long-absent feathered, furred, and scaled creatures of the marsh make their appearance on land and in the water and skies.

THE RITE OF RETURN

APRIL OFFERS UP many de-
lights, none so exotic as the
return of wood ducks.
Seeing a pair cruising upriver by the house, I call to Cathy to
"come quick."

"Wood ducks. Have a look."

"They're so beautiful," she exclaims, peering through the
scope.

"Haven't you seen them before?"

"No."

I remember seeing my first male wood duck and the sense of
wonder—verging on the transcendental—that it inspired. I was
at the pond, below the garage where the driveway made its wide
swing to the road. Feeling somehow that I was being watched, I

turned to see the multicolored bird perched in the alders. When it flew, I ran as fast as my legs would carry me up the hill and burst into the kitchen, breathlessly trying to describe to my mother what I had just seen.

"A wood duck," she smiled.

How do you describe a wood duck to the uninitiated? It seems best expressed in poetry, whose purview is beauty. Prose is always trying to tell us something, whereas poetry wants to show, not tell. Decades later, I wrote a poem about that first encounter with a wood duck:

> At the pond muddling for minnows
> I looked behind, suddenly aware
> of the watcher—there, perched in alder,
> was the wood duck. A Noh play actor
> with its green warrior's helmet,
> white facial lines pencilled on
> like those of an ancient mandarin.
> Back and breast anointed in irreverent purples,
> visceral maroons, metallic flashes of iridescence
> like dragonflies embroidered on silk lamé—
> such an oriental extravagance in the grey world
>   of drab April!
>
> I did not quite believe it to be a bird,
> but an altered reality winged as angels.
> Reverence hushed my breathing, stillness
> strained to hold its beauty;
> then I moved and the bird vanished,
> as if a tree hole were the portal
> to another world,
> some brightness beyond nature.

April

Darwin observed that "birds appear to be the most aesthetic of all animals, excepting, of course, man, and they have nearly the same taste for the beautiful as we have." But he found the showiness of male birds a challenge to his theory of natural selection, as such beauty seemed to make them more vulnerable to predation and therefore was an impediment to survival.

Female birds are mostly dull creatures, adopting cryptic coloring as camouflage so as not to attract attention to themselves or their young. However, they seem to have an eye for the beautiful in the male of the species. Thus, Darwin argued the reason for the male's showiness, and the vulnerability it conferred, was to be found in a mechanism he called sexual selection. Being bright and beautiful allowed males to mate with more success and therefore pass on their genes. For the male bird in breeding plumage, it is a balancing act between vulnerability as a result of being conspicuous and fertility as a result of displaying one's attractive qualities.

Experiments have shown that various creatures are attracted to exaggerated forms even if they rarely or never occur in nature—a phenomenon dubbed the supernormal stimulus. Thus, a male fritillary butterfly will reject a female to pursue a mechanical model that has bigger, brighter, and more rapidly moving wings. Male geckos will display to a photograph as large as a billboard. Edward O. Wilson summarizes this supernormal response this way: "Take the largest (or brightest or most conspicuously moving) individual you can."

The imperative of reproduction aside, what we find beautiful, aesthetically, often equates with strangeness—at least in my mind. The wood duck, cosmetically, is unlike any other duck in the pond. It is uncharacteristically showy, it is supernormal, and we immediately pick it out from the rather drab crowd. Although I am a confirmed Darwinist with no faith in the Creationist concept of a Divine Watchmaker, the wood duck drake almost appears designed rather than evolved, it is so strange. Regarding this most beautiful of our ducks, it might seem evolution is both a practical and an aesthetic tinkerer.

RARITY IS STRANGENESS of another kind—quantitative rather than qualitative—but sparks a similar thrill in the watcher.

In early April, with snow still covering the marsh, I see something strange, unidentifiable. My first thought is "fox": a ruddy color against the snowy backdrop and the bushy tail trailing luxuriantly. But when I consult my naturalist's journal, I discover a glaring absence. Foxes, with the exception of a single year, are nowhere to be seen in April.

Also, the animal plows through the knee-high snow with a heaviness to its movement, not the light-footed grace of a fox. The mystery animal lumbers along, head down, its hindquarters scissoring forward, the way a bear might run. A raccoon? But where is the dark coloring, the striped tail? There are no stripes, and although this animal has the posterior heaviness of a raccoon or a bear, it is too large for the former and too small for the latter. It is an animal, I conclude, I have never seen before.

Then it stops in its dash across the marsh and sits upright on its haunches, like a groundhog. But at this size, a meter (3½ feet) tall, it is no groundhog. After it disappears behind the trees, I must go to my books. Through a process of elimination, I conclude that I have seen a fisher, a rare sighting, which will not be repeated in the years to come and perhaps never again in my lifetime.

No wonder: fishers are an endangered species, extirpated by trapping from much of their range in Nova Scotia and New Brunswick by the 1920s. They were reintroduced from Maine into western Nova Scotia in 1947 and again in the 1960s, apparently successfully. But a remnant native population has survived in Cumberland County, where I live. Still, they are so rare that my septuagenarian neighbor, Sherman, a trapper and woodsman all his life, has never seen one.

Ironically, fishers don't fish. Their name is the North Americanized version of the old Danish word *fitchet,* meaning "to stink," applied to polecats in the Old World. Like all members of the weasel family—skunks, otters, weasels, and badgers—fishers have well-developed anal glands that they deploy for both communication and defense. They mark their territory at breeding time but reserve their most potent anal musk for situations in which they are threatened.

Before that April day, I knew it only by reputation as a porcupine eater. The fisher circles its quilled quarry, biting at its head until the porcupine is immobilized. This formidable predator then flips the porcupine on its back and attacks its unprotected underbelly. The porcupine cannot escape by climbing a tree, as the fisher sports semiretractable claws for tree climbing. Occasionally, of course, it gets too close, and fishers have been known to die of quill wounds.

Thanks to Henry Ford, fishers' ecological function of controlling porcupine populations has been taken over by cars, which came into their own around the same time fishers were disappearing from the native fauna. Fortunately, these rare and beautiful animals are making a comeback as their predators—humans—pursue them less diligently.

TRUE TO T.S. ELIOT's pronouncement, in Maritime Canada, April is often a cruel month. There are intimations of summer, but rafts of ice linger stubbornly in the strait, stirring Arctic onshore winds, accompanied by a slurry of snow and freezing rain. It is, in the local idiom, "mud season."

In the muds of the marsh, however, a tough survivor of this tidally ruled environment, with its constantly shifting conditions, has taken root. The delicate seeds of the saltwater cordgrass, *Spartina alterniflora,* have been broadcast over the marsh muds the previous fall. In order to germinate they need a prolonged cold period—amply provided by winter past. But they also require dilute salt water, which spring rains and river runoff now furnish.

Cordgrass leads a double life: above ground it is an annual, perpetuating itself by seed production, while below ground it is a perennial, depending upon rhizomes (roots) to sprout new growth. It is this latter means of vegetative reproduction that is by far the most important. Much of the surface growth of the plant has been, as we have seen, removed by the actions of the ice and tides, but the rhizomes continue to push themselves through the mud, knitting the marsh soils together and giving rise to new shoots in spring.

Over the coming weeks, I will scan the marsh intently for any signs of green. The greening of the marsh is incremental, slow but inexorable, like the coloring of a copper roof by a green patina. Another even more subtle plant growth is occurring on the surface of the muddy banks of the river and tidal creeks and on the exposed muds of the marsh itself. Rather than a "greening," this transformation is best described as a "browning."

The slurry at the surface of mud—a zone where water, air, sunlight, and nutrients mix—provides all the necessities for the production of life. The newly exposed muds are now slick with microscopic plants called diatoms. These tiny plants are surrounded and protected by a two-piece silica shell, a glasslike casing that functions as a solar greenhouse, capturing carbon dioxide and sunlight, which, combined with the minerals and nutrients in the marshland soils, power a proliferation of these vital algae. Over eons, they can accumulate to form geologic strata hundreds of meters thick and are the source of much of the petroleum sequestered in the Earth. In the living system of the marsh, they are food for many marine animals. Blue-green algae, spreading on the muds between the cordgrasses, add another important pulse of productivity in spring.

And in the marsh pools, or salt pans, filamentous algae and pondweed flourish under the longer daylight hours, setting out a green buffet for the ducks that are funneling up the eastern seaboard, along the Atlantic flyway. The first to arrive are the black ducks. For their tribe, the salt marsh is an especially important feeding ground. They make their appearance as pairs, or in small flocks, as soon as there is open water, feeding around the *aboiteau* and later, when the snow and ice has cleared from the marsh, progressing to the marsh pools, where they tip up to glean the pondweed reaching toward the light.

These are big, chunky ducks—macho ducks—conspicuous even at a distance. They are the ducks I spied from the dormer windows of the farmhouse when I was a child and, I now think, were probably the first birds I could call by name. They were also the first waterfowl I tasted when my father or brothers were lucky enough to bag one on the marsh. Their succulent flesh melded the rich tastes of their diet of mussels and snails, aquatic plants, and wild grains and grasses. They stayed all winter in the Chebogue River, which never iced over. Looking out from the high windows of the farmhouse, I could see their silhouettes any month of the year.

Here, two degrees latitude farther north, they return in the spring, either on their way to more northerly breeding grounds or to nest in local marshes, including the Old Marsh. They are followed quickly by other marsh ducks—blue-winged teal and green-winged teal alight on the marsh pools, their white rumps flashing as they tip up in the intense spring light. These little ducks are the spitfires of their race, jumping straight up on takeoff and fleeing with disarming speed and maneuverability at any threat—the shadow of a harrier, eagle, gull, or raven passing overhead.

Come April, I too am restless and, following my own migratory urge, drive down the coast to the mouth of the next important river, the Shinimicas. The estuary is also surrounded by generous strips of salt marsh but, unlike the Tidnish, has no cottages lining the bank. The diversity of waterbirds that gather here sparks a kind of ornithological spring fever.

I park my car on the Northport wharf, where fishing boats are tied up, awaiting the opening of the herring and lobster seasons, still a few weeks off. I walk up to the bridge that crosses the Shinimicas and, taking out my Minoltas, scan the water up and down the river. Upriver, there are perhaps a hundred black ducks, monochrome in the listless April light, and a lone great blue heron feeding. Seaward, there is an impressive flock of brightly patterned ducks, which I identify as common goldeneye. There are perhaps two hundred birds, male and female, in this "raft." At this distance the distinguishing feature of the male is not its namesake eye but the green-glossed head with a prominent white spot before the golden eye. The males are mixed in with more drably marked females whose white neck ring is barely visible above the chop. The males throw back their heads so that the top of their heads touch their wings, an exaggerated posturing I deduce is designed to attract the attention of the females in the flock. They dive in unison. I count, "One, two . . . ten . . . twenty" seconds, before they emerge, bobbing up at last like Ishmael's coffin life-buoy. Mixed-in are red-breasted mergansers. Their

April

crests flare out at the back of their heads like bad hairdos from the 1950s—in the idiom of the day, a "duck ass." A low murmur, a gabbling, rises from the water, like the crowd sound on a movie set, where, I understand, extras are instructed to mumble, "Rhubarb, rhubarb . . . "

As I scan the flock, I can pick out another species of bay duck, greater scaup, which emits its namesake call, *Scaup, scaup,* a cacophony that reverberates over the ice-studded waters of the bay. These hardy birds will remain along the coast all winter, wherever there is open water and food. In spring they begin to congregate in estuaries like the Shinimicas. Before April is out, they will be gone, winging to their northern breeding grounds, around James and Hudson bays, the Magdalen Islands, Anticosti Island, and Newfoundland. For a few fleeting days in April, I can find them here, diving for molluscs and adding their nasal pitch to the dissonant duck chorus. The goldeneyes, too, will go north (though not as far) to find natural nest holes in boles or stumps of mature trees, which may put them in competition with wood ducks for nesting places. They will sometimes lay their eggs in another goldeneye's nest, a behavior known as intraspecific brood parasitism. This behavior may be driven by a shortage of suitable nest sites, a situation aggravated by the logging of large trees that provide natural nesting cavities. However, a parasitized female may compensate for the cost of raising "adopted" offspring by laying more eggs if she detects eggs in her nest that are not her own.

The goldeneyes and scaup are only here for a few short weeks, during which I feel compelled to renew our acquaintance. But I am not a "twitcher," that dedicated breed of birder who, for example, frequents sewage lagoons in search of a rare bird. And I have never kept a list, except for the informal one that has emerged from my marsh journal. But I must confess to a certain satisfaction in knowing where and at what season to find certain species, like the common goldeneye and greater scaup. "There you are, just as I thought," I say to myself as I swing my binoculars through the flock. This emotion is not so smug or acquisitive as it might seem, so much as it is comforting, a reassurance that all is right in the world. If the sea ducks and bay ducks return to the estuary, and the marsh ducks and dabblers come back to the marsh, as predicted, then I know the ecosystem is functioning: phytoplankton is blooming, mussels are filtering this microscopic fodder, and ducks are fattening. The circle of the seasons is revolving as it should. The pattern underlying the cycle of life is intact.

Record keeping, I admit, reveals some curious symmetries. A pied-bill grebe shows up on the river the same day—April 23—in three separate years. (I experienced a flutter of delight as I checked back through my entries. The recognition of such patterns, such rhythms in nature, is somehow pleasurable to humans, reminiscent of the pleasure I derived from looking at the repeated arabesques in a threadbare Persian rug that graced our dining room floor on Brook Farm.) It works the section in front of the *aboiteau,* like so many other waterbirds, for it is here that the marsh delivers its most concentrated load of nutrients. Detritus eaters, zooplankton, and fishes all gather here to take advantage of the marsh's outpourings. The marsh acts as a great sponge, absorbing the waters of the incoming tides. When the tide retreats, it begins to drain, and the drainage is continuous until the next high tide. Almost any hour of the day or night, I can hear the trickle of water coming off the marsh and with it a steady stream of nutrients—a process marsh biologists call outwelling.

The grebe is a primitive bird in the evolutionary scheme of things, just above the loons phylogenetically. With my study window open, I can hear its muted loonlike warbling between dives. I also observe its curious defensive behavior of sinking so that only its head sticks out of the water, like a periscope. In April, breeding season, it sports a distinctive whitish bill, with a dark bill ring—thus, "pied-billed." It is a dainty, whimsical-looking bird, almost chicklike, and I am always disappointed when it soon moves on to find a breeding ground on a freshwater marsh, where it will build a floating nest, near shore. The salt marsh and tidal river are way stations only, stopovers while the grebe waits for the freshwater marshes to thaw out.

THROUGHOUT APRIL, the winged fishers return, led by the great blue heron. The herons usually arrive singly, but one morning I look out to see not one, not two, but six herons stalking a marsh pool in tight formation—the most I have ever seen at one time on the Old Marsh. It must be a flock; the birds must have migrated together and are dining now that they have reached their destination. This number of great waders bespeaks an almost equatorial richness. To a bird, they have a crisp look in their newly minted plumage.

I return to my writing, but when I look up again, all of them have struck a perplexing pose, with their necks craned skyward at 45-degree angles, their bills upthrust, as if they were looking up, in alarm. In their coordinated precision and posture, they look like soldiers shouldering arms. All six march toward the tree line and hang about in the shadows of the spruce. Inexplicably, they have abandoned their feeding ground en masse. Could this novel behavior be some kind of mating ritual?

Still later, the herons do an abrupt about-face, downriver, and then I see why. A bald eagle cruises in to perch on top of a spruce. At his approach, three of the herons take off; one continues to cower in the trees, refusing to take its eyes off the potential predator, while its remaining companions stare out at the marsh, perhaps testing their nerve. But they do not dare to venture into the open.

For now, it is a standoff between these titans of the marsh, until a crow buzzes the eagle and it flies off. Now that the danger is past, the herons relax their outstretched necks, hunching their heads between their shoulders as if their dignity has been damaged.

THE BLUE HERON was the timekeeper of my childhood days on the marsh. Our biological clocks seemed to tick in synchrony. When I ventured forth on a morning, the gangly silhouettes of herons arriving at their feeding grounds trailed overhead, appearing mysteriously out of the fog that usually draped our marsh world until midmorning. (We sometimes applied the inelegant but venerable term "shitepoke" to these graceful gliders, which described the way their straight legs seemed to be rammed into their posterior when the birds were in flight.) As the daylight hours waned, I would see them again, departing the river, headed to some distant island nesting ground. Seeing them flying home, I knew it was time to return to the house and supper.

I once surprised one while it was intent on feeding, poised over a marsh pool. I walked right up to it before either of us was aware of the other. It is hard to say who was more surprised, or frightened. At a bit over a meter (roughly 4 feet), the great bird was as tall as I was then, and we regarded each other eye to eye. Its gold eye was hypnotic, betraying no emotion; its beak, a gilded dagger. It was as if I had slipped into a cosmic wormhole and found myself in the Eocene, a time when the *Titanis,* or "terror cranes," ruled the earth. Neither of us wanted to take our eyes off the other, adversaries locked in a mortal gaze—but finally it flew off, as my heart beat audibly against my thin chest.

April

DAILY THE HERONS fish the marsh pools and river shallows, stalking on their long legs. Their precision and patience is that of a poet searching for the *mot juste*.

One strides through the shallows with a deliberate bent-knee stride, leading with its beak, its eyes like pince-nez. It stands motionless for minutes on end, until a fish swims within striking distance. The heron hunches its long S-shaped neck between its shoulder blades, then lunges, uncoiling its neck and plunging its head underwater, seizing the fish in its wedge-shaped beak. After swallowing, the heron always shakes its great hoary head, then continues its vigil. Sometimes I count its successes—one, two, three, four, five; it rarely misses, though young birds are less successful than the more practiced adults. I contrast my own feeble attempts to catch a minnow bare-handed, despite the finely tuned reflexes with which I was endowed as a young boy.

The other expert fisher is the well-named belted kingfisher, a study in the alternative fishing methods evolution has devised. Like a blue heron that has been compacted for aerial hunting, it has lost its long neck and legs but retained the heavy, scissoring head. (In fact, the belted kingfisher is the sole member of its family in North America and is unrelated to the great waders.) It is similar in color—a slate blue with ruddy wing patches—and has a similarly large daggerlike beak. There the similarity pretty much ends: the kingfisher has a short, thick footballer's neck balancing its oversize head—to absorb the shock of its dives—and extremely short legs with small syndactyl feet (two toes partially joined) adequate for perching. It may dive from a perch or hover and dive, plunging headfirst into the water, even into the shallows of a marsh pool.

Perhaps because of their consummate fishing skills—to which I aspired—these two birds have fascinated me since boyhood. From spring through late fall, I saw herons daily and never tired of their impressive size and grace. My memory of belted kingfishers comes from a single reel, played over and over again. The family would take Sunday drives, often to fish for trout. My father was as devoted a fisherman, as I myself have become. At the head of the Chebogue River, we would pass a salt marsh and a creek, and there was always a kingfisher perched on the telephone wire, ready to dive. The image is indelible: the tufted, massive head, the compact form, the cobalt blue. I looked for that kingfisher every time we drove by. Without recognizing it, I was beginning to develop an ecological sense, to know what creatures I could expect to see, when and where, and to understand what they might be doing there—the kingfisher on its wire waiting to dive for minnows shimmering through the salt marsh grasses.

ON A MID-APRIL morning, I am walking the dog when I see a swirling motion in the narrow creek that crosses the road. "More smelts," I think, having seen the first of the spring run enter the creek mouth a week before. They have been amassing there, waiting for the spring tide to breach the culvert and allow them to swim up the tiny freshwater brook that is their native spawning ground. But at the end of the swirling motion, a dark form emerges—an otter, eagerly devouring the smelts that he has trapped against the lip of the wooden culvert.

Otters are superb fishers, equipped as they are for an aquatic lifestyle—possessing dense fur for repelling water, webbed feet, and capacious lungs to support long dives. Their large, crushing molars make them a formidable foe, capable of killing mink and, it's believed, even beaver in their lodges. They are, moreover, intelligent creatures, which none can doubt who has observed them at play or catching fish.

April

The otter chomps through one smelt after another, until he notices me, mere meters away, and beats a hasty retreat toward the river. I feel bad, having inadvertently interrupted his meal, but I know that he will be back to finish his repast. When I stop to talk with Sherman at his mailbox later that morning, he shakes his head: "Well, I never. Never seen them do that before."

The little brook that drains into the creek is not unlike the one I knew as a boy on Brook Farm. It rises in wetland, runs parallel to the ship railway, then drains through one of the railway's intact sandstone culverts before meandering through a little wooded ravine to the creek and the Tidnish River. I can easily step across it in most places. When we settled here, I posed the question "Will smelts run the brook?" and was rewarded that first spring when they did.

On the farm smelting was a rite of spring, a ritualistic act that seemed to be essential to the turning of the season itself.

In April I would amble down to the marsh to keep watch for the schools of smelt then about to enter the creek. These small fish are an estuarine species, living for most of the year in brackish waters, where they form an important feedstock for seabirds and commercial fish species such as cod. But once a year they must enter fresh water to spawn and reproduce.

From a bank above the creek, where pasture spruce shaded the water, I kept watch daily for the smelts' reappearance. From my hiding place among the evergreens I could spy on the black schools of smelt amassing at the mouth of the brook without spooking them. The nervous fish would not enter the brook to begin their annual bacchanal until nightfall. Under cover of darkness, my father, brothers, and I would slip like mink to the creek bank to intercept them.

My father had already prepared for that night. He had stripped the bark from an alder to make a sturdy net handle.

With rabbit snare wire, he bound a metal hoop to the tip and tied a porous, red onion bag to the ring to complete the dip net.

In our rubber boots and spring jackets, we traced the path to the creek, the bent, frost-tinted grass shining in moonlight. We used flashlights to locate the fish, furtively scanning the water and averting the beam immediately when we saw their bright bodies and luminescent eyes flash back. Dad manned the net, dipping downstream into the thick schools and emptying the fish onto the marsh, where they contorted in the damp grass, then lay still, magenta and silver under the moon. I kneeled below him on the bank and plunged my hands into the dark, icy waters. Feeling the rough scales of the fish flowing by, I grasped the smelts and flipped them over my shoulder, then plunged my hands in again until they were numb with cold. It was a frenzy, as when whales or seabirds spot a mass of fish, knifing and diving through them. Then it was over—the fish either having retreated into deeper water or slipped by us upstream.

We gathered the catch into burlap bags and climbed the hill, wet and happy and strangely tired as the excitement drained away. Mom had stoked the stove in anticipation of our arrival, and the kitchen heat hit us like the opening of a furnace door. She cleaned the fish in the sink, her tiny, red-knuckled hands— worn by butter churning, baking, and weeding—working the scissors, decapitating the little fish, and slitting open their bellies, spilling the milt, eggs and guts into a bucket (they made good fertilizer for cucumber hills). Rolling the fish in cornmeal, she filled two large cast-iron frying pans. The room filled with the onomatopoeic aroma of smelt. Although by now it was well past my bedtime, no one mentioned it. Even on school nights, I was allowed to stay up for this communal feast, the sweet white flesh falling away from the bone and dissolving in the mouth. This was the taste of April.

April

Weeks later, when I began my eel catching in the brook, I would lift a stone and the decomposing corpse of a smelt would roll up and drift downstream to fertilize the ocean. For some the imperative of spawning had ended in a natural death. But each spring the smelts returned, despite our carnage and the *extremis* of reproduction.

We fished only one night, taking enough fish for a feast. Now I realize that our spring rite was not legal. There was a prohibition against smelting at night (which we always did because of the wariness of the fish), and in the 1950s there was a limit on the number of fish you could catch, as there is today. Stealing toward the marsh, net in hand, we kept a lookout for car lights, which might signal the approach of a fisheries officer. Once, a suspicious RCMP officer confronted my father while he was walking on the salt marsh during smelt season, asking what he was doing there. "Can't a man walk on his own land?" Dad replied in his cryptic manner.

There is obvious peril to exploiting fish stocks on their spawning grounds, as commercial exploitation of the northern cod has tragically shown. Dragging their spawning schools has driven this greatest of all North Atlantic food stocks nearly to extinction. The predator, however, finds it hard to resist the opportunity such a congregation presents. The otter had risked coming up the creek to the roadside to take advantage of the trapped smelts. One spring, not long after we moved here, the neighborhood kids, including my daughter, got carried away with the fun of catching smelts, bare-handed as I had as a child, in the upper reaches of the little stream. It was several years before this small population returned to spawn in any number. I felt the sting of guilt in giving in to nostalgia and letting them have their fun, as I had, without first instilling a proper conservation ethic.

And I gave a sigh of relief when I saw the smelts once again amassing thickly in the creek.

I NOW EXPECT TO SEE otters in April, fishing for smelts and cavorting on the riverbank.

A pair appears at the *aboiteau,* sporting in the outflow. They dive repeatedly, crushing their prickly-looking prey—either rock crab or sculpin—in their powerful jaws. Their gregariousness is beguiling: one balances on the other's back with its front paws, gazing about with a look that can only be described as curious. It then climbs onto its playmate's back, and, lying one on top of the other, they slide down the tenacious shore ice like children sledding. Their movements seem so synchronous, as if they can read each other's thoughts—like a practiced ballroom dance team.

Two days later I see this pair again. At first I think it is a large bank beaver with its back humped above the water. But then I discern it is a male otter riding its mate's back, locked in a coital ballet, a kind of carnal synchronized swimming. There is no thrusting, no frenzy, as the two swim in tight circles. With each turn they submerge, sending up soft bubbles of air, and then emerge *au pair,* snorting air. There is no struggle, no panic, as they slowly tip to one side like a listing boat. Their movements in lovemaking are as graceful and sensuous as all otter movement—sliding down a bank, diving, or swimming, the paragon of sleek grace. What is so mesmerizing and, I suppose, so unotterlike is the leisurely pace of their lovemaking. I first spy them at dusk and watch them until the light fails, as they circle, turning round and round, over and over.

It is a rare and beautiful thing, the reward for staying in one place and keeping watch. Travel yields diversity; residence, intimacy. Staying in one place, looking and looking while the seasons rotate around you, reveals the patterns inherent in the familiar. It is like an experiment repeated over and over again, until some reproducible truth is teased out. Probability becomes an ally that in time reveals the sublime, snares the evanescent.

April marks the time of return for many migrants—of wood ducks and sea ducks, of fishes and the winged and furred fishers who depend upon them. They are following the arabesques of their annual migratory paths, north to south and back again in spring. Throughout this continental shuttling, I remain in one place, ever watchful, looking for both the familiar and the exotic, the commonplace and the rare. Like the boy reading the Persian rug, I try to piece together the patterns that define this place.

5

May

A RUSH TO LIFE

Pi-ta-wee-pi-ta-wee-wee-wee . . . The willet's cry, more than any other sound in nature, strikes a physical chord within me. My body vibrates in sympathetic response. Like tuning forks and tides, the call sets up a resonance. As it did when I was a child, it says to me, "I belong here." That was how I felt when I heard a willet careering over the Old Marsh on our first day in our new home: improbably, in midlife I had found my way home after a long, circuitous journey.

Of all the creatures that I encountered in the languid, salt-tinged summers of my childhood, none moved me more than the willet. Its territorial cry seemed to also proclaim my very own piece of earth.

I wheeled, following the sound, and squinting into the sun, I picked up the silhouette of this swift shorebird planing in for a landing on the marsh. It lit on a hummock and, as willets always do, raised its dark wings, exposing the bold white chevrons on the undersides. We do not know why willets make this grand gesture, but to me it was the visual equivalent of their cry—another yes to the question, "Is this home?"

In May the shorebirds are whistling north, answering to the hormones in their blood and the compass in their brains. Killdeers arrive first to scout out their breeding territory, circling the marsh and crying all the time to ensure that potential mates will notice them—as if they could be ignored. They will nest in my neighbor's meadow, in a shallow scrape. Yellowlegs follow soon after, tall on their yellow stilts, sure of themselves, raising a racket with their constant *keek, keek, keek,* which is shriller than I can make it sound in print. Within days, the willets will demand to be heard, throwing a lariat of sound around the marsh.

There is another shorebird sound in the spring skies, a whooping, phonetically rendered as *huhuhuhuhuhuhuhuhu.*

I am walking the dog over Charles's blueberry field, only a week after the snow has melted. As we circle the field, a snipe jumps up from a drainage canal, fluttering away with quick beats of its dappled wings and rising over the marsh, where it drops its haunting call.

Henry David Thoreau called it "a spirit-suggesting sound." It is an uplifting hurrah, for sure. When I was a boy, this ululation sounded to me like the war cry I made by baffling my mouth with rapid hand movements while uttering a long "whoo."

I remember walking out on a spring evening and hearing this vibrato above the sodden pastures of Brook Farm. I looked up to see, silhouetted against the darkening night sky, a snipe frantically circling, as if it had been sucked into a vortex of air. Snipe circle 30 to 60 meters (100 to 200 feet) above their territory, then dive headlong at a 45-degree angle. As they plummet toward the earth, they fan out their tail feathers at right angles to the body, causing them to vibrate in the onrushing air. The movement of the wings, superimposed on the tail-feather vibrations, creates the birds' characteristic winnowing and a haunting sound. Climbing, circling, and falling—it is all part of the male's territorial display to attract a mate. To the nineteenth-century transcendentalist, the sound of a snipe was that of a sky spirit; to a naïve 1950s boy, an echo of a Hollywood Western. And in South America, it is likened to the ripping of a shroud, the voice of the dead speaking beyond the grave.

I have another association with the snipe's nuptial song, mixing sound and smell—in memory. In spring, just about the time the snipe returned to their breeding ground and it became warm enough to cast off my winter clothes, I might get a new denim jacket, or as we called it in the country, a dungaree jacket. The smell of denim dye—indigo—was potent. I wore this new jacket proudly on the first warm nights in May. Now, years later, the sound of a snipe always smells blue.

MAY IS A HEADY MONTH, almost disorienting in its richness. Every living thing seems to sense how little time it has to accomplish its mission—to reproduce. There is a rush to life everywhere I look. There is no common day on the marsh, a day when something remarkable does not pass before my window view, but this is more true in May than in any other month. The salt marsh grasses push up with the urgency of asparagus. I am convinced it would be possible literally to watch them grow—

perhaps even to hear the cells dividing—if I had the patience of a child and the freedom to sit in one place with no agenda other than to see and hear what is happening around me.

The morning begins in mist. The water is, as Sherman says, "calm as a clock." A black duck opens a silver seam in the marsh pool; a green-winged teal makes its clear call, like a high-pitched penny whistle with a pea rattling in it; a killdeer *keeks,* far off; an osprey rises like a Chinese kite over the tree line with nesting material trailing from its hooked beak; a convention of yellowlegs poses on the marsh islands like decoys, bills tucked under their coverts; willets wheel by, garrulous as ever, winged calliopes playing the fanfare of a marsh day in May. The semipalmated sandpipers, or "peeps," skim the marsh, creating a mesmeric pattern of dark and light as they bank and whirl, guided, it seems, by some group intelligence so that they appear to act in flight as a single organism. A lone great blue heron stalks a marsh pool, and a resident kingfisher spins in the air like a flywheel before plunging into the pool, which is popping with minnows. It carries back a silvery prize to its nest, dug about 1.5 meters (5 feet) into the riverbank.

A muskrat cruises upriver carrying sprigs of marsh grass to line its burrows in the drainage canals that exit at the *aboiteau.* And a lone bank beaver—a huge animal, probably 20 kilograms (45 pounds) or more—chugs up and down the river like a tugboat. Like the muskrat, it will make its summer home in the bank of one of the drainage canals—unlike the beavers upriver, which will construct traditional lodges from saplings, backing up the streams that flow into the main river.

When Sherman still hayed the Old Marsh, in May—the only month of real spring in Maritime Canada—he would repair the dyke, sealing breaches with new sod, which he cut with a long-handled sod knife. He would also inspect the canals, jamming sod into the muskrat and beaver burrows to prevent clogging of the canals, which would impede drainage of his marsh hay field.

THE VIXEN TAKES UP station on a driftwood log to survey her domain, looking longingly at the waterfowl feeding there.

Pairs abound. On any given May day, there are pairs of American black duck, green-winged teal, blue-winged teal, common pintail, and American widgeon commingling on the marsh and belted kingfisher and osprey engaged in aerial courting displays. I watch as a pair of blue-winged teal initiates its courting with a series of head bobs, a kind of courtly bowing one to the other, a ritualized nodding of assent. The act itself, however, is a rather crudely practical, one-sided affair. The male maneuvers behind the female, mounts her, and seizing her roughly by the nape of the neck, pushes down on his mate as if to drown her during the abbreviated coitus. Seconds and it is over, and the two go their separate ways, performing postcoital ablutions, consisting of much wing beating and splashing.

There is an odd couple on the marsh, a female American black duck and her dapper consort, a mallard drake. The mallard, like the wood duck, is a supernormal duck, with its strong coloring—a glossy green head and a white ring around the neck. To compete, the American black duck male has only a royal purple wing patch to brighten its otherwise drab brownish plumage. Females, it appears, prefer the showier mallard, a trend that is a cause of much consternation among conservationists and hunters. Mallards have long been domesticated, and the strong coloring of many domestic ducks belies their mallard ancestry. Most numerous in the Prairie provinces, mallards were so rare in Atlantic Canada as to be an oddity fit for mounting at the turn of the century, and the few that did occur in the wild were considered escapees from domestic flocks. But wild mallards have been steadily moving eastward with the spread of corn and grain growing. Now they are widespread, at the same time that black ducks are diminishing in numbers.

Despite the rather dramatic differences in appearance between the two males, they belong to the same species. The phenotype—the look of the animals—is different, but their genotype—their genetic makeup—is the same, opening the door to interbreeding. Black duck females now tend to prefer the foppish mallards as partners, consigning the black duck drakes to the status of cuckolds. Bright and flashy does make it in nature, as in show business, it seems. Looking out at the marsh, in my backyard I am witnessing a drama of genetic subterfuge, of one race slowly supplanting another.

Life is also quickening in the estuary and the bay as light floods the water column, boosting the growth of phytoplankton and zooplankton, which, in turn, nourish the filter-feeding shellfish and fish species.

Scores of cars and pickups string out along the shore road this time of year, a sure sign of the "clam tides," spring tides that lure diggers onto the flats in search of the prized bay clams, or quahogs. The waters of the Northumberland Strait are shallow and subject to small tides of little more than a meter (3½ feet), but at the ebb tide people are spread out across the mudflats and wading chest-deep in the water, a half kilometer (about a third of a mile) from land. Burnished by the setting sun, the scene always reminds me of Impressionist landscape paintings; the humans along the strand are subordinated to the mauve, rose, and golden light playing on the water and sand.

In summer, the strait waters may reach 28°C (82°F), making them the warmest waters north of the Carolinas. These conditions have preserved a fauna here more typical of the coast south of Cape Cod. There are extensive oyster beds at the mouth of some rivers, where seasonal fishers tong them from flat-bottomed boats. There are also large beds of razor clams and, of course, quahogs.

My introduction to this wonderful, bottom-dwelling fauna came when I was eleven, during the one extended trip that my family made in the Maritimes, to attend my oldest brother's wedding. The family had crossed over the mouth of the Bay of Fundy by ferry from Digby to Saint John, in New Brunswick, then drove on to Moncton. After the ceremony, we crossed over into Nova Scotia via the Tantramar Marsh and then drove to Pugwash, 40 kilometers (25 miles) from my present home in Tidnish Bridge. We were visiting relatives of my mother's mother, who lived at the mouth of Pugwash Harbour on the Northumberland Strait.

We arrived late in the day, and faced with the prospect of listening to adult talk, I made my escape to the shore as soon as was politely possible. Among the jetsam I found a cornucopia of, to me, strange shells and other never-before-seen marine creatures.

There were sand dollars aplenty. The tops were incised with a perfect five-petaled pattern, and below, five, pie-shaped plates met at a central hole, the mouth. In the living creature (an echinoderm), the upper surface is covered with dense brownish red spines, fringed with hairlike cilia, which move microscopic food to the margins, then to the mouth. Tube feet, or podia, account for the petal pattern on top. They are not used for locomotion, as in other echinoderms, such as sea urchins, but have been modified for breathing.

In the specimens I found that day, all spines and feet had been worn off, however, so only the bleached, pockmarked shell, or test, remained. I stuffed my pockets with them, as if they were doubloons. There were razor clams whose 18- to 20-centimeter

(7- to 8-inch) shells looked like the handle of my grandfather's straight razor. They were sharp, too, and brittle, but I found room for them in my bulging pockets. There were delicate slipper shells; turning one over, I saw that inside there was a platform, covering half of the shell. (This so-called deck gives them their other common name, boat shell, though I knew nothing of this, only that I had never seen one of these fragile shells before, and I popped it into my pocket.) And perhaps most wondrous of all, there were moon snails the size of baseballs.

I doffed my sneakers and socks, rolled up my pants, and waded into the shallow waters. There I saw living moon snails, each plowing through the sand on its great foot. Again, I did not know it at the time, but these slow-moving predators were hunting down clams, which they engulf with their foot; then, boring a hole through the shell, they suck out the live animal. I also saw the egg cases of this great snail, collared with sand particles, without knowing what I was observing. And blue mussels attached to the base of rock weed and rock crabs scurrying through the shallows.

The sun was down by the time I made my way back to the house. My pant legs were wet and smeared with mud, my pants pockets bulging with treasures, my sneakers sodden. I must have looked like a disheveled Robinson Crusoe, thrown ashore on a remote, godforsaken island, though inwardly I had the glow of the discoverer of a wondrous new land, like a young Darwin visiting the Galápagos for the first time.

I FIND A PARKING PLACE and, donning my hip waders—always in the trunk during trout season—make my way across the flats toward the distant figures. A cold wind is blowing across the water as the sun sets. Wading in, I note two large, bluish moon snail shells, and new eelgrass, a brilliant green, which in the longer daylight hours has already grown several centimeters.

I see a young man trailing a green plastic carton tied to his belt. Such a man knows what he's doing; he has a system, I think, and I join him. He is a young fisherman from the community whom I recognize, though not by name.

His name is Darren, and I quickly learn as I follow him through the shallows that his newborn son has just arrived home from the hospital that day, yet here he is on the flats. It is a compelling business, this clamming for quahogs.

"What do you look for?" I ask, thinking of soft-shell clams, which I have often dug. "Holes?"

"No, shit like there," he says, pointing to fecal pellets the size of cake sprinkles, "but bigger."

As we wade along, our eyes watering as they focus through the shallows, he calls my attention to a blue starfish, smaller than my palm. Suddenly Darren bends over and plucks from the flats a "razor fish," as he calls razor clams. He gives the shell a squeeze, forcing out the white meat.

"They're some good raw," he says, swallowing. "Really sweet."

The razor clams leave a deep impression, the size of a quarter, and are much more numerous than the sought-after quahogs. The latter can grow to 15 centimeters (6 inches) in diameter and are becoming increasingly scarce, so much so that local people petitioned to have commercial clam diggers excluded from the flats.

"They cleared out Seaview," he says with disgust. "Filled up two or three boxes each. Took them out by the wheelbarrow, even. It's not sustainable."

Darren tells me he likes to eat the quahogs steamed or ground in a chowder or, best of all, "jarred," that is, pickled.

May

"I like them in the winter, eating them out of a jar watching the hockey game," he says. "I just want enough for myself and my wife."

I learn that earlier in the day, he and his father have set out thirty-two gill nets, and at four in the morning he will be on the bay pulling in herring for sale to the smokehouses in the nearby Acadian village of Cap-Pelé.

THE LOCAL POPULATIONS of herring have dropped in recent years, but some springs the herring still mass in large schools in Baie Verte, feeding on the zooplankton and fish larvae proliferating there. I keep an eye on the bay coming and going from the country store, turning off the Jackson Point road and driving by the winter-deserted summer cottages to the shore. When the herring are present, I often see great white birds with black wingtips circling the bay. They fold their wings and plummet like missiles, sending up explosions of spray. They are northern gannets that have stopped off here to feed on their way to Bonaventure Island, off the tip of the Gaspé Peninsula, or farther north to the great gannet colonies of Newfoundland and Labrador.

Like the albatrosses, these great seabirds can glide over the wave tops, sometimes for hours, without ever beating their 2-meter (6½-foot) wings. This "wave hopping" employs the natural updrafts off each crest. It is their daredevil diving, however, that elicits the greatest admiration. Like most predatory birds, such as owls and hawks, the northern gannet has well-developed binocular vision: its eyes are positioned toward the front of the head, so the visual fields of each eye overlap to a degree. This trait enhances depth perception and allows it to estimate how far below the surface its prey lies. It has no nostrils, and its upper and lower bill fit tightly together to prevent ingestion of water on hitting the waves. Most important, it has a system of air cells between the skin of its neck and shoulders and the muscles beneath. Upon diving, the gannet inflates these cells to cushion its body and head from the tremendous force of impact. The dive drives the bird below its prey, and it swims upward with its wings and webbed feet to capture the herring.

I watch these great birds circle and dive for as long as I can withstand the biting winds whipping the bay into whitecaps.

THE MARSH IS GREENING before my eyes. The creek bank and dyke are respectively spiked with *Spartina alterniflora* and *Spartina pectinata,* the spear-shaped grasses sticking up like green pike poles beside medieval moats; the central portion of the Old Marsh—technically, the high marsh where the tide floods only intermittently—is carpeted in the finer *Spartina patens.* Last year's salt hay is still a tousled, russet mat, whipped into cowlicks by fingers of wind. But day by day, the salt marsh grows greener, transformed by the sun's energy into a seaside oasis. "Look at how green the marsh is," Meg exclaims, arrested by this annual miracle.

No less awed by the wonder of this transformation, I nevertheless attempt, in a reductionist manner, to trace the stages of this marsh makeover. This, then, is how the marsh goes green: first, *S. pectinata* atop the dyke turns grass-green; then *S. alterniflora* along the canals, a yellow-green; finally, *S. patens* rimming the marsh pools, a darker, forest green.

The colors this time of year are as delicate as haiku: the new verdancy of white birches, the fire of red maple skirting the marsh edge, limning the delicate pinks and whites of dogwood as subtle as an Oriental screen. From behind this panel of May color emerge the first fox cubs of the year.

May

This is the spring event our household has been keenly antic-
ipating. I can hardly wait until Meg and Cathy get home to announce, "We have babies."

As long as we have lived here the White Birch Foxes have
produced a litter every year but one. Their den, bracketed by
the sylphlike sentinels of two white birches, is directly across
from my window view when I am at my desk. To the side and
closer to the marsh lies a spruce deadfall and a tangle of driftwood brought in by the tide, which we call the playpen, for it is
here, under a protective canopy, that the fox kits begin to learn
about the wider world.

The foxes have been absent, at least from my view, throughout April. This is when the litter of fox cubs, on average five, are
birthed and remain with the vixen in the leaf- and grass-lined
den. They are born blind, their eyes opening during their second
week. Only then will the vixen venture out to hunt; during
these times the dog fox may guard the den. After a month
(around the first of May in our part of the world) the cubs
emerge from the den under the watchful eye of the vixen, or
sometimes of both parents, as the dog fox often takes part in the
rearing of the young.

I keep a close eye on the den to make a head count of the
year's litter. Over the early days of May, one cub after another
emerges into daylight. We have had as many as seven and as few
as three. They greet the world as tawny roly-polies, cushioned
by a generous layer of baby fat from mother's milk. They continue to nurse, but in the coming weeks they will, under their
mother's guidance, learn to hunt and, through their rambunc-
tious puppy games, harden to the challenge of survival that
awaits them.

The vixen is a doting mother, indulging the nursing cubs,
suckling, nuzzling, and preening them. In our time here, we

have come to know two vixens: White Face and her daughter Black Socks.

White Face brings this year's litter of four cubs out to catch the evening sun. It is to be her last litter. When I first spy them, they are suckling, all four at once, poking at her teats aggressively. Mother stands patiently, like a cow attached to a milking machine, but soon tires of this rough treatment and tries to walk away. Two cubs follow behind and again nuzzle her. She suffers them for a moment but again moves off and lies down on the edge of the marsh to take her ease in the low rays of the dying sun—the very picture of the harried mother who has had enough care giving for one day and wants only to collapse on the couch while chaos circles around her. The cubs, however, still have energy to burn, and pairing up, they attack each other head to toe, chewing on each other's ears, feet, and tails until one retreats, only to be tackled again, starting a new round. Occasionally, one tires of this roughhousing and disappears into the playpen.

Soon one of the cubs reappears, this time dangling a still-bloody groundhog pelt in its mouth. White Face has brought this plaything back to the den to instruct her brood on how to hunt. This way, the cubs learn the smell of prey and begin making the conversion to meat eating. The little fox shakes the pelt fiercely like a family dog playing with a favorite old sock. This attracts the attention of the others, who, each seizing a corner of the bedraggled carcass, engage in a tug-of-war.

White Face, who has been overseeing these antics, now decides to go for a ramble along the edge of the marsh, mounting the dyke as a lookout. Three of the cubs follow, straggling far behind, while the other, less brave one sticks close to the den. The vixen keeps watch from the dyke until dusk, while her young return to the playpen. She seems little perturbed by our presence across the river; she does not even react when our dog begins to bark for our attention.

Foxes are inured to human disturbance, which has helped them to survive the incursion of that larger canine—the coyote—into their territory. Coyotes avoid humans, denning far from human habitation. Often I engage in staring matches with the White Birch Foxes. The river divides us, which must be some comfort to them, and I avoid crossing to the marsh when the cubs are still about so as not to unduly disturb them. Our family takes too much pleasure in their presence to risk trespassing on their territory.

Cathy, Meg, and I have grown uncommonly attached to the White Birch Foxes, protective in the way one is toward a family pet, I suppose. Our world would feel incomplete without them. I was particularly fond of White Face. I cannot say I came to know her, but we did have a relationship, a consciousness of each other and our separate places on either side of the river and marsh.

A larger divide separated us: my self-consciousness and her, to me, unknowable inner reality. "The closest we come to actually touching the interior of another animal is through the eyes," writes theologian Gary Kowalski in *The Souls of Animals*. More than once, White Face and I looked into each other's eyes, I with growing affection and she . . . well, all I can say is, with acknowledgment. As I knew her, she knew me as an individual, one whom she did not have to fear.

I did not grow up with a sentimental attitude toward animals, domestic or wild. It was an emotional luxury we could not afford on the farm. We slaughtered chickens and pigs, though they and the cattle were not subjected to the "desacrilizing"—to use a term coined by Kowalski—conditions common to modern factory farms. Their lives, for the most part, were clean, free of stress, and good. As needed, we hunted, trapped, and ate wild animals in season.

Later, during my studies in biology, I served as a lab assistant in an animal physiology course where frogs were sacrificed— relatively painlessly, by first destroying the central nervous system, a procedure called pithing—to demonstrate metabolic processes such as muscle contraction. And after graduation, I was a research assistant at the Ontario Veterinary College on a project designed to produce a vaccine for feedlot cattle. The work involved reproducing neurological disease in animals and performing autopsies on those few that succumbed. Although such experiments are designed to benefit humans, and animals in this case, Kowalski points out that they not only rob animals of their "holy qualities" but are dehumanizing for us.

101

I will always carry the moral burden of these experiments— but it has not robbed me of my compassion, and, paradoxically, may have strengthened it. On May 13, 1998, I recorded an encounter with White Face in my journal:

> *I saw White Face this evening at dusk. I am always delighted to see her—the little thrill of recognition of her as an individual, coupled with the relief that she is still alive, has made it through another winter. She stopped for a few moments to regard me, our mutual gazes suspending us in a ritual of acknowledgment and acceptance. But I was shocked by her appearance. The white face reminded me of the pallor of the dying, that kind of transparency that seems to attach itself like a mask to those about to cross over the limits of this world. She broke the trance, moving on with purpose and disappearing over the rim of the dyke.*

I saw her only one more time, two weeks later, in the rain. She was mud splattered and bedraggled. There were no kits that year.

THE LIFE SPAN of a fox in the wild is surprisingly short. Few live more than three or four years, though they have the potential to live twelve years. The White Birch Foxes have survived on the edge of the marsh for as long as Sherman, in his late seventies at the time of this writing, can remember. The year following White Face's death, there was a litter of seven cubs, the most we have ever seen. I took special delight as Black Socks moved the den closer to the playpen of her childhood, where each spring since a new litter has appeared in the first days of May.

The foxes come out daily, weather permitting. Usually I see them in the morning or evening, rarely singly. Black Socks allows them greater leeway as the days advance, and she also leads them on feeding forays on the marsh, teaching her charges the fine art of stalking. She jumps off all fours, landing on her two front paws to pounce on a meadow vole, or perhaps only imaginary prey, and the cubs imitate her, hopping like little jacks-in-the-box.

As the month advances, I notice she has less patience with their need to nurse. They are far from able to provide for themselves, however, so she continues to provision the den.

Late in the day Black Socks returns, dangling a large snowshoe hare in her jaws. I haven't seen the cubs all day, but on hearing their mother approach they pop up from the den, like gophers, one after the other, and set upon her—all seven. She drops the rabbit and flees into the den, five of the cubs in hot pursuit. The two remaining cubs immediately begin to tangle over the hare. This is not one of their mock fights but an earnest effort to establish dominance. They bite each other on the back as they tumble together; finally, one retreats, while the victor tackles the hare. I see the great hind feet—the unlucky rabbit's feet—sticking into the air, as the dominant cub gorges on the softer body parts. Eventually, another skirmish ensues, and the other cub wins this time. Later the other kits take a turn at dissembling the hare, except for the runt, who cannot hold his own against his brothers and sisters and probably is doomed as a result. Finally, our little foxes are bloodied and sated. One cleans its chin on the ground, wiping its mouth of the gore on the marsh grasses.

I develop a sentimental attachment to the runt, probably because I occupied the same position in my family, as the youngest and smallest. He stays closest to the den and his mother. Like the little fellow, I was also the stay-at-home, never wanting to leave the farm, seeing no advantage in doing so, as all I wanted—birds and brooks, fish and freedom—was to be found there.

The cubs grow more independent as May advances. They are turning redder, as the marsh grows greener, presenting an ever-more pleasing picture as they play their dog games, romping through the high grass. They stray farther from the den now and are no longer constantly under their mother's watch. Soon they must fend for themselves. They have few natural enemies, but a dog, coyote, or bobcat might kill a fox if given a chance.

One morning a pair of Canada geese planes over the marsh and, seeing new grass, lands to crop it near the playpen. The geese attract the attention of one brave cub, who, in hunting mode, crouches low and begins to stalk the great birds, which more than overmatch him in size. He advances, then retreats warily, never venturing onto the open marsh itself. He keeps to the protection of the woods, believing, I suppose, as young animals (including children) often do, that he is somehow invisible. The geese are well aware of his presence and, apparently, not very concerned about it. One acts as a sentinel and occasionally honks a warning, stretching up its long neck to keep watch for the vixen, though I wonder whether even a mature fox would have a fighting chance against these great birds. This pair feeds at its leisure before flying off, unharmed.

Lesser waterfowl are in more danger, however. Ducks nest near the marsh at their peril, and among the food items Black Socks brings to her young is an American black duck. I identify it by the purple wing patch. I remember, too, finding whole wings—no bodies—on the marsh edge as a child. I never connected their mysterious presence with foxes; if they were present, I never saw any.

MAY IS A TIME OF RENEWAL for all living things, a sanguine time. Like the little foxes, the trees take on a ruddy hue as sap is drawn into their budding branches. A small flock of purple finches alights in the apple tree, which is a mare's nest of new growth. The males with their rosy breasts cling to the branches like early ripened fruit. The winds buffet them, rocking them up and down on their perches so violently you might think they would get seasick. As I observe them more closely, I can see why they are so tenacious. The tree is not simply a roost, a port in the storm, but their garden. These ruddy silviculturists are pruning the treetop, literally nipping it in the bud. They are eating the new growth as it emerges. I wonder what effect this has on the tree's growth—perhaps it is as beneficial as humans' more heavy-handed pruning? Sometimes the purple finches are joined by American goldfinches, which local people call "canaries." Later, when the blossoms burst forth at the end of May, cedar waxwings (their wings apparently sealed like an old-fashioned letter by a dab of red wax) will suddenly appear to eat the pink-and-white blossoms. Even so, the old tree that divides our property from our neighbor's will yield more large, if sour, apples than we can use in the fall.

Land birds arrive in waves all month: chipping, Savannah, fox, and song sparrows come early. I wake to their *sweet, sweet, sweet* music. By midmonth, the ruby-throated hummingbirds are back. These smallest of our birds have come from as far away as Costa Rica, homing perfectly to their birthplace. What is more remarkable is that they demonstrate a very specific knowledge of this place.

I am coming through the breezeway one May day when I am met by a male ruby-throated hummingbird. He stalls in front of my face, within an arm's length, chattering loudly—in a furious temper, it seems—before shooting off to the spot under the eaves where the feeder should be hung. He hovers there, as if to say, "Haven't you forgotten something?" He shuttles back and forth a couple more times just in case I have missed the point. What is most astonishing is not that he knows where the feeder should be but that he obviously recognizes my role in replenishing it. Within his pea-sized brain he has logged the nature of our special relationship and is able to communicate it to me—in no uncertain terms.

The swallow clan—barn, cliff, and tree swallows—is also back, swooping over the river and marsh, hawking down the insects that are hatching under the warming days.

Everything is a verb in May: swallows swoop, snipe winnow, ducks mate, and songbirds sing. It is in late May that I take what I call my warbler walks. I have not been back to the ship railway since the mud replaced the melting snow. There is an expression in the Maritimes: "There is one day between the snow going and the mosquitoes coming." It is barely an exaggeration, but there are a few days in May before the mosquitoes become overwhelming when I can walk the railway in comfort, looking for warblers. The lack of mosquitoes makes this a pleasurable pastime, and the lack of leaves on the trees allows me to identify these brightest of our feathery visitors. By the third week in May, "leaves are as big as a mouse's ear," goes the old country saying.

Because I do not have the ear of an expert birder, I must see the birds to know which ones have survived the contemporary threats of pesticides and deforestation and the age-old perils of migration to return to the north woods. (Warbler populations have declined by as much as 20 percent in recent decades.) For the most part, it is the male birds that sing, feathered Carusos belting out their love songs in an effort to attract a mate.

Bird song has been described as "protomusic." While simple and repetitive, it contains all the basic elements of human-made music: rhythm, tones, harmony, and melody. Such pleasing songs have a biological function: to attract a mate. But birds also appear to sing to please themselves. How else to explain the persistence of singing, even outside the breeding season? Perhaps they sing for the reason versified by Gerard Manley Hopkins, "myself it speaks and spells"—the avian equivalent of "I think, therefore I am."

Whatever their motive, the warblers' songs draw me into their sensual world, one dominated as much by sound as by sight. The warblers' high-pitched notes, rising and falling in glissando, remind me of the virtuoso playing of Dizzy Gillespie. Though surely less complicated than jazz riffs, they project the same exuberance. Alerted to their hiding places by their singing, I spy northern parula, magnolia, chestnut-sided, pine, and Nashville warblers in the trees, their little heads thrown back, beaks in the air like Gillespie's upturned trumpet. Another day I see a yellow and a blackburnian warbler (that little ball of fire, aerial cinder) and a drab little fellow, a Tennessee warbler. As I walk along, my head cocked back, absorbed in bird song, I don't at first notice that I have been following along in bear tracks.

THE SOUNDSCAPE is often as important to me as the visual field in making me aware of what is happening in my environment. Through the open window, I hear crows raising a ruckus in the direction of Charles's blueberry field. Through the scope, I can see a murder of crows scavenging a carcass on the riverbank. I decide to investigate. The cause of this commotion proves to be a porcupine. It is tipped on its back, and the viscera have been expertly removed. The exposed skeleton, shining through, has a pinkish sheen and almost looks plasticized, while the back still bristles with quills. I wonder whether this is the work of the fisher I had seen in April and the crows have merely arrived to finish the job. There is no way of knowing for sure. So much of life's drama goes unseen and must be reconstructed from the little evidence we discover after the fact.

May is a mixed chorale of shorebirds' harsh calls, warblers' more tuneful offerings, and the competing whistles of osprey and eagles as they circle the marsh. But perhaps the surest sign of spring's advent is the shrill piping of tree frogs—peepers—that begins as night falls. Not even birds sing with the unrestrained joy of these amphibians. Their high-pitched register seems to set the marsh vibrating.

On a warm evening late in May, Cathy and I walk through the darkness to the dock and stand there in our pajamas, listening to a primal chorus that reaches back through the eons to a time when there were no mammals and no birds, to a time before the first diminutive ancestors of the great dinosaurs trod the Earth. This is the night music of spring and an anthem to evolution. We listen a long while, until the night chill descends. As we make our way back to the house, June bugs splutter out of the grass, crashing blindly into the clapboard.

6

June

A TIDAL CLOCK

OUR FIRST YEAR ON the river, I hear a telltale whistling through the bathroom window and rush outside for a look at a magnificent "fish hawk" at work—forgetting, in my rekindled enthusiasm for the varied life of the salt marsh, to turn off the basin tap. The osprey stalls above the river, hanging in the air, then folding back its boomerang-shaped wings at an acute angle, dropping, checking its free fall once on its way down, then striking. Talons thrust forward, it plunges, igniting an explosion of spray and reemerging with a fish held headfirst in its claws. To enjoy its meal, the osprey repairs to a tall pine at the corner of the marsh, perching atop the tree like a weather vane, its white head and mottled, pale belly visible to my naked eye.

When I return to the bathroom, the water is just cresting the basin rim.

In June the river begins to fill to overflowing with gaspereaux making their spawning run en masse, tens of thousands of these freshwater spawning herrings, a living, silvery tide. The gaspereaux dimple and splash the normally placid river surface with such ardor I can hear them stirring the waters through the open study window late at night as I lie in bed across the hall.

During the day this massing of protein attracts the constant attention of the marsh's most formidable winged predators—osprey and bald eagles. I see them with gaspereaux gripped in their talons, light glancing off the fishes' silver scales as it does off the distant, sunstruck fuselages of overflying jets. Osprey are the most conspicuous fishers during these gaspereau days; sometimes three or four at a time tower on thermals, circling the marsh and following the river course to zero in on their target. Their high-pitched whistle, like a ship's sonar, pierces the summer silence.

For all its speed and power, the osprey is no match for its prime competitor, the bald eagle. The eagle would rather fight than fish, however, and I often watch as one harasses an osprey until the "fish hawk" releases its prey, whereupon the eagle swoops down, catching the gaspereau before it hits the water and whisking it away, a behavior known to biologists as kleptoparasitism, or avian piracy.

Over the years, eagles and osprey scooping gaspereaux from the river and marsh pools become a familiar if still-remarkable sight. What I witness one day comes as a total surprise, however, as it has to every other naturalist and biologist to whom I have related the story. The osprey soars low over the marsh, banks in a tight hook over the *aboiteau,* fanning out its tail feathers and driving forward with its talons. This precision move takes but seconds, and when the osprey accelerates again, with hardly a moment's hesitation, it has in its talons a fat young muskrat. The victim doesn't struggle, though I can tell it was alive because its tail wags—a most pathetic reflex. The osprey must have killed it on impact, driving its talons into the muskrat's vital organs. It is a devastating display of killing efficiency, which perhaps explains the origin of its common name from the Latin, *ossifraga,* literally "bone breaker." The osprey seems to fly off with little effort, disappearing upriver to provision the brooding female in her nest.

GASPEREAUX ARE an important link in the estuarine food chain, setting the table for a diversity of predators. This member of the herring family goes by a variety of common names: sawbelly and crazy fish, but most often, alewife. I grew up calling these sweet but bony fishes "kayak," a designation derived from the Mi'kmaq and used exclusively in southwestern Nova Scotia. Later, when I attended Acadia University, in the heart of the Land of Evangeline, I was introduced to *gaspereau,* a French word that gave its name to a river valley not far from the campus, under the South Mountain. In late spring, the gaspereaux throng the river of the same name, where fishermen-farmers have been catching them for generations. They set square nets in the river and keep watch from a plank catwalk above a platform (called a stand) built out from the riverbank. When one sees the fish schooling over the net, he jumps on a boom, swings heroically down like a swashbuckling pirate, landing on the stand, and with his body weight counterbalances and lifts the net, flipping with silvery fishes. They are pickled in salt and exported to the Caribbean, a tradition that goes back to the golden Age of Sail in nineteenth-century Nova Scotia. Then, these bony fishes were traded for Jamaican rum, hardly a fair deal, it seems, and one that epitomizes the hard-bitten reputation of Nova Scotian sea captains and traders.

As a boy I accompanied my father to inland rivers where the kayak were making their way upstream (though kayak ran in the Chebogue River, our brook was too small to provide spawning territory). Mostly Acadians fished this species, which, because of its extreme boniness, was scorned as table fare, at least by those who could afford not to eat it. The fishermen wielded large dip nets—beautiful things made from black spruce poles and a black cotton twine netting—from stands erected beside sluiceways built by piling up river stone. A long catwalk from the shore, spanning shallow runs, led to the stand, and I had to place my feet carefully on the slippery, precariously balanced boards to avoid falling in. At dusk, verging on darkness, under the roofed stand, olive-skinned men talked in a sharp but musical language I did not understand—but for the odd English phrase or curse.

Perhaps for the first time, I became dimly aware of my own foreignness. For generations in southwestern Nova Scotia, the English had lived side by side with the French—in my family's case, since 1785—but our communities had remained culturally separate, divided by language and colonial history, just as the Chebogue River divided us geographically. My Acadian friends at school always spoke English, admonished no doubt by their parents to "fit in" and by unsympathetic school authorities who, in the 1950s, were decades away from embracing bilingualism. Now I heard my Acadian playmates' fathers speaking their native tongue as they dipped their black nets into the black waters. But the very rocks we stood upon might well have been piled by another people, the Mi'kmaq, who built stone fish weirs to exploit this fish run—one that reached back to a time when the glaciers were just receding from the continent's edge and these rivers were unpeopled.

Flashlights and hurricane lamps lit up the corners of the weathered, open-sided shed. Iridescent fish scales sequined the floors, the walls, and even the ceiling as the fish were dumped into barrels, where their throes beat the rainbow armor from their dying bodies. Those that were not eaten would be salted and sold for lobster bait. Weeks later, when my father and I returned there to fish trout, a few dried scales still clung to the gray boards, the funky smell of spawning gaspereaux still emanating from them.

THE YOUNG FOXES appear morning and night and forage for themselves now. Their coats have taken on the mature red of the adults, which is as conspicuous as a British army tunic, a dead giveaway against the intensely green backdrop of marsh grasses. On high tides some of the gaspereaux swim through the *aboiteau,* over the inundated marsh, and into the marsh pools. I see them circling there, dorsal fins out of water, creating concentric wakes as they stir up plankton from the muddy bottom while feeding. When the tide drops, they are trapped and become easy pickings for osprey or, as I discover, even terrestrial predators.

One evening I look across the river to see a fox cub with a gaspereau clamped in its jaw. The fish seems oversize only because the fox cub is still so small. The little fox is overmatched by the fish, which is very much alive, flapping its head and tail vigorously in an effort to escape its captor. Seeming not to know how to react to the fish's unwillingness to become supper, the little fox runs for the woods but soon reappears with the gaspereau still protesting vigorously. Finally, the fox drops the fish, whose belly is furnished with sharp, saw-toothed scales—a rude discovery I made as a boy when I tried to pick up the "crazy fish" and its razor belly scored my palm.

JUNE IS OFTEN a rainy month, and the marsh then is an electric green under a cobalt blue sky. Three blue herons struggle into a heavy wind. It is a primitive spectacle, transporting one to the Jurassic, when skies must have been filled with such great, gawky creatures.

June rains fuel the marsh's greenery, the sun's fire expressed as riotous growth. This bounty of marsh grass always brings out the deer. I look up and suddenly there is a deer, red as a fox, in its luxurious pasture of spartina, belly high and, in places, shoulder high. This event is entirely visual, soundless as a dream. The deer, for its part, is all ears, which are erect, rotating and twitching to detect any untoward sound. The marsh grass has tempted it into the open, to savor its nutritious new growth, its essential salts. The deer is torn between the succulence of the grass and its own safety, and I can see through the scope, by the twitching of its ears and flank muscles, that it is exercising a great deal of willpower in not panicking at the car sounds, which travel clearly across the river to where it grazes at the marsh edge. Finally, its instinctive fears overcome its momentary pleasure, and it bounds into the security of the woods, the warning flag of its white tail held high—the dream dissolving.

At this time of year, I may see a young buck, its vibrant velvety horns gathering a halo of light around its head. (Once, on an island in the Labrador Sea, a young Inuk cut off the tip of a caribou antler with his hunting knife and, peeling back the velvety covering, fished out a piece of pale yellow marrow and offered it to me as a delicacy. It tasted salty and had the consistency of toffee.) Or a doe, her udder full. I know her fawn lingers somewhere nearby, camouflaged in the tall grasses or forest edge, where its spots blur into wildflowers or blooming shrubs. In time, when the grasses reach their full height, the doe will bring her charge onto the marsh.

It is a dead calm June morning with the tide just high. Only the willet's cry breaks the peaceful spell cast by such a breathless day. On Lucius's Marsh, a large doe stands in the belly-high spartina. She is an extremely long animal, majestic in her red summer coat, which glistens in the sun, every muscle shining, taut as a thoroughbred, finely tuned and ready to run. Then I spy through the lattice of grasses another brown shape, a fawn bounding behind its mother. When the fawn stops, I can see only its tiny tail twitching above the grass tops—a nervous wand telegraphing, I surmise, a happiness at being in the midst of such richness.

I, too, had this feeling as a boy in the midst of the marsh, the green world enfolding me. Every day at high tide, I would go with my mother to the marsh creek, where she would swim. I usually sat on the shore watching the tiny fishes filter through the flooded stalks of marsh hay. Sometimes I would dog-paddle to the middle of the narrow creek, where there was a rock I could anchor myself to. I was a bony boy, with no natural buoyancy, so swimming never came easily to me.

In contrast, my mother, herself a mere 40 kilograms (90 pounds), was a natural swimmer. She coaxed me into the water, holding me gently under the belly and, when there was enough depth, released me, whereupon I thrashed for shore or the safety of the rock. I could not have drowned, and knew this, but I feared the water nevertheless.

I don't know why I suffered such a primal aversion, but looking back, there might have been a number of reasons. A boy my age, in the community across the river, had drowned. Or perhaps my fear was ancestral: my fisherman grandfather, Jeremiah Reede of Cape Sable Island, had been lost at sea, his dory swamped by a February storm, and neither his boat nor his body was ever found. Still, my mother, who had been given up for adoption by her destitute, widowed mother, had learned to trust the water. Then, a young man in our community had caught his foot in an anchor rope and been pulled to his death in the river, near where we swam. My father, too, was a nonswimmer. But for whatever reasons, I frustrated my mother's gentle efforts to coax me into the water. I was in my twenties before I forced myself to overcome my childish fears and became a swimmer.

Care seems suspended on this June morning. I am a child again, watching the doe and fawn move lazily through the high grasses, the doe looking up from time to time to see that her child has not strayed. Finally, however, the highway sounds unnerve her and she stamps her front foot to alert the fawn that it is time to flee, and they hightail it away together.

In June the young take their first steps or brave the air or the water. Hidden somewhere in the woods, the black duck has made her nest and raised her brood. By midmonth she is ready to bring her gold-cheeked ducklings to the marsh, to teach them the ways of water.

She chooses a day of torrential rains to do so, reminding me of my mother's saying, "Only ducks and fools go out in the rain." Mother Black Duck may be a duck, but she's no fool. She has chosen this day for her brood's baptism precisely because no other creatures are about to bear witness, in particular Mother Red Fox, who, with her four cubs, has been cavorting around the marsh every good day and evening but is now hunkered down in her den. Eight downy ducklings follow their mother in obedient single file and, one by one, into a marsh pool for a swim—no doubt their first.

Later in the day, the rain abates and the vixen appears. One cub accompanies her a short way but then turns back to the woods and the comfort of the den. The vixen lies low in the tall grass for five minutes, then skirts the woods and advances along the far southeastern corner of the dyke. She has picked up a scent, the trace of the duckling entourage, and makes a beeline for the marsh pool where I last saw them. She comes forward, foxily, with purpose, slinking low to the ground. Suddenly, a spotty sandpiper jumps up and sounds the alarm. It seems to put Mother Red Fox off her pursuit, blowing her cover, and she beats a hasty retreat to her brood's playpen. The ducks, I think, might not be so lucky in the future, now that the fox knows to be on the lookout. Four fox kits and eight ducklings: the sad arithmetic is that most, predator and prey, will perish in the coming months; most will starve or be eaten.

OVER THE YEARS, I notice that very high summer tides present exceptional feeding opportunities.

When a tempest forces the tide a meter (3½ feet) up the lawn, I must go out and tie down the dock to prevent it from floating away. There is virtually no land visible on the marsh, just the top of the dyke here and there. Tree swallows flock over the dyke top, feeding on mosquitoes and insects forced out of the grass by the rising waters. The swallows' wings beat—*flick, flick, flick*—like frames in an old-fashioned movie reel as they strain against the prevailing wind. There must be a bonanza of ephemera for the swallows to battle such winds and come out ahead, energetically, for they stay and fight the wind as long as the tide delivers.

Barn swallows feed from the surface of the river in a roller-coaster ride, gliding low over the water, dipping their beaks into it—barely kissing it—snatching emergent insects just as they break the surface tension of the river, and then rising up with a few quick flaps of their blue-black wings.

After we built our River Room onto the back of the house, a pair persisted in trying to build a nest at the peak of the 5-meter-high (16-foot-high) roof. They begin by building a small mud shelf to serve as the foundation for their nest. Work goes slowly at first, but they finish their job in a flurry of activity on a single day when high tide is at 7:50 A.M. The timing, I realize, is significant: the tide is dropping all morning and is low for much of the day, exposing the mudflats along the river-bank. All day, the pair flies to and from the area of the *aboiteau,* dabbing at the soupy mud there and bringing back tiny pellets to apply to their growing nest. By evening, when Gary arrives for supper, they have nearly completed a bowl-shaped structure, which is cemented to the soffits on either side of the peak.

I take Gary out to show him the nest builders' progress, which inevitably sets us talking about the swallows that every year built one nest, or frequently more, under the eaves of the garage and on exposed beams inside.

"Dad never knocked them down," my brother recalls.

"I think you're right."

"He also left the garage door open during nesting season so that they could come and go. I can remember having to duck as they went in and out."

Inevitably, one or the other of us would find nestlings where they had fallen from the nest. They were the most pathetic crea-tures I have ever seen—nearly naked, gray, gape-mouthed, with desperate eyes filling their oversize heads; the only visage more disturbing is that of a starving child. I would take these birds in-side, cradling their pitiful bodies in my palm, and improvise a nest from a shoe box lined with cotton. We tried to keep these emaciated nestlings alive by feeding them white bread soaked in warm milk—never successfully, of course.

"Why didn't we feed them insects?" I ask my brother.

"Maybe we didn't know what they ate," he says.

As we grew older, we continued to try to rescue these doomed birds, knowing full well our methods never succeeded. Such was the compassionate nature of our fatalism. But our failure was not so different from the many more sophisticated interventions by humans in the natural world.

For the next three days, a strong, steady wind blows from the southwest. I check on the state of the nest, now regally presided over by its owners, their heads and tails appearing jauntily above the mud walls.

On the morning of the fourth day, I go out to inspect the nest, only to find the shattered remains on the ground. It looks like a broken pot, an artifact at an archeological site. I pick up a large piece of this "potsherd" to examine it more closely. The outside is rough and knobby, made so by the little balls of mud the swallows apply. I find a strand of wool in one piece, perhaps intended as reinforcement, and in another a few pieces of eelgrass. But what is most remarkable is the inside, which is smooth except for the minute marks made by the swallows' beaks as they finished the walls of their home like master plasterers. The little marks most remind me of the cuneiform writing of the Sumerians, especially as it, too, was inscribed in clay.

Despite this disaster, the little birds begin rebuilding. The tide is high at noon, and as it begins to drop, they go back to work, shuttling to and from the *aboiteau* and the roof peak, dabbing at their mud palette like painters mixing their oils. What bright optimists, I think, as I watch their exuberant, lyrical flight, rising and falling as in a musical line, and listen to their cheerful chatter under the eaves.

Tragedy strikes again, however. Three days later I find two swallow wings below the nearly completed nest, the body gone.

I suspect our great white tomcat, Gris, must have caught one of the swallow pair as it veered too close to the deck railing. The nest site is abandoned and not rebuilt this year.

SUMMER IS FULL of bird talk. The whistling of the osprey and eagles continues throughout the month of June, as long as the run of gaspereau lasts. It is a time of plenty for these great fishers, and I think to myself, why shouldn't they appear happy at their work? The steady fish supply feeds their young secreted in treetop nests upriver, ensuring another generation.

Other sounds echo up and down the river, including the un-mistakable quavering of a loon. Its plaintiveness is also justified, at least in my mind, as this is likely a nonbreeding bird passing the summer in salt waters; breeding pairs occupy inland lakes (usually one pair to a lake). Then there is the sound of an Ameri-can bittern, which cruises into the marsh on a rainy day. In flight, he might be mistaken for a blue heron but for his slightly smaller size. He lands in the tall *Spartina alterniflora* and begins his curious stalking. In his drab brown plumage, he is like an ec-centric old gentleman inspecting the marsh. He crouches and hunches toward a marsh pool. Finally he takes up his station, craning his neck skyward—this most ridiculous of birds!—in imitation of the tall grasses. Despite its dubious dignity, this form of camouflage is effective.

The strangeness of its mating call outdoes even its behavior. The bittern's common name is stake driver, after the sound a stake makes when driven into wet ground. Hearing it, I imagine the ghost of some pioneer Acadian returned to the Old Marsh to reinforce a crumbling dyke. The male's mating call also reminds me of the sound of an old-fashioned hand pump, such as we had in our kitchen on the farm, gulping air when it was being primed with a small tin pan of well water my mother kept next to the sink. It is a wet sound, guttural. To produce it, the bittern contorts its neck horribly, puffing it up like a bullfrog, then swallowing—upward—forcing air through the outstretched pipes of its neck and into the summer silence. He calls all night and the next day, too, seeking to attract a mate with this unappealing performance.

The bittern will not nest here, however, but on a freshwater marsh, a few kilometers away, where on early summer nights I sometimes stop to listen for this odd fellow cleverly hidden among the cattails. If I follow the same dirt road deeper into the woods, I will come to a drowned forest. Tree swallows nest here in the tenements of the bare and weathered boles, riddled with nest holes. There are hundreds of these slate-backed birds weaving through the air of this avian neighborhood and gossiping to their neighbors from the stoops of their high-rise homes, in a joyful communal conversation. Some of these same birds must be the ones I see skimming over the dyke top of the Old Marsh, having traveled overland for a windfall hatch of salt-marsh mosquitoes.

But in June, the most persistent bird talk belongs to the willets; for shrillness and sheer garrulousness, they have no equal.

All day a pair of willets raises a racket in vigorous defense of their territory—obviously, in their minds, the whole marsh. They unleash a blitzkrieg on the trespassing crows, creating a virtual no-fly zone above the marsh, sunup to sundown. They will not even tolerate a crow perched on the far side of the river. They plane between the trees, swooping up to mount another dive-bombing attack on the hapless crows, all the while spewing forth a constant volley of alarm calls, in the skies and on the ground. Returning to the driftwood perch by the *aboiteau,* they are soon off again, harrying the crows or a kingfisher when it leaves its riverbank nest for a feeding foray over the marsh pools, and, brazen birds, even harassing ravens and eagles. Their message is simple, consistent, and unrelenting: *Keep, keep, keep away!*

All of this commotion raises my hope that the willets are nesting nearby, not just vigorously protecting a feeding ground. Willets usually nest within a hundred meters (320 feet or so) of a salt marsh, sometimes in small colonies of four to eight pairs. Their nest is nothing more than a shallow scrape, a hastily improvised swirl of vegetation, often hidden under a low bush. Robie Tufts writes in his classic *The Birds of Nova Scotia*: "A nest containing four eggs was found at Chebogue concealed under a clump of blueberry bushes . . . " I wonder exactly where he uncovered the nest, thinking maybe it was at the base of a prominence we called Blueberry Hill that sloped toward the marsh and the Chebogue River.

I did not know at the time how privileged I was to have willets as companions to my childhood days on the marsh. Plump, presumably tasty, and fearless, they had been easy targets for hunters since colonial times, and so by the turn of the century the only place they were presumed to breed along the entire eastern seaboard, north of the Carolinas, was on the salt marshes of southwestern Nova Scotia where I grew up.

The willet's presence there was established by Harrison F. Lewis, who was to become the first director of the Canadian Wildlife Service. He was also the eldest son of one Reverend Gordon Lewis, from whom my father had bought Brook Farm. It was with some pleasure, then, that I read, on a fragile, yellowed copy of *The Auk*, Vol. XXXVII, 1920, from the archives of Acadia University:

> *My own experience with Nova Scotian Willets is practically confined to the lower valley of the Chebogue River, in Yarmouth County, where on the extensive salt marshes and the neighbouring*

*upland fields and swamps, Willets are not uncommon, as I have
known since 1911, if not earlier.*

At the time, Dr. Lewis must have been staying with his father
at Brook Farm, and must have written up his field notes under
the same high roof where I spent my boyhood, like him, sere-
naded by willets.

Daily, I walk the dog downriver and around Charles's blueberry field. As I approach the far end of the field, where on
spring tides the salt water inundates my walking path, a pair of
willets takes exception to my presence. Their strategy is passive-
aggressive—alternately decoying and attacking. One of the pair
flies up and perches on a slender alder, displaying its wings with
the white chevron underneath. The treetop bends under its
weight, as it hurls a screed of protest on my head: *Keep, keep, keep*
away; it hopes to distract me. Meanwhile, its mate circles, hurl-
ing itself at my head and swerving away at the last moment; its
intent is to repel.

I feel I must be close to the elusive nest that year after year I
search for in vain. I look under the willow bushes and larches
that like this marshy soil (local people say, "They like wet feet").
I rein in the dog in case we get lucky. We don't, however, even
though I keep up my search on my daily walks. The willets have
done their job well, not only in defending their nest but in hiding it. In a month, the young will add their voices to the chorus
of cries corralling the Old Marsh.

Harrison Lewis was a much better nest finder than I have
proved to be. He found at least two willet nests that long-ago
summer, in June 1920. He uncovered the first "in an open swale
in an upland pasture . . . on the western side of the Chebogue
River," and a second "at Cook's Beach, at the mouth of the

Chebogue River." With obvious fervor, barely constrained by his scientific duty, he described the nest in detail:

> *The nest was scantily lined with dry grass and "eel-grass" and was in a slight hollow on top of a dry grassy knoll, about fifteen feet above the high-tide mark, which was about fifty feet distant. The sitting bird was surrounded by short growing grass and strawberry plants, and by two or three small plants of Iris. It flushed from the nest at my feet, and by loud cries attracted its mate and its neighbours, so that I soon had the pleasure of seeing six Willets in the air together near me.*

Our first summer on the marsh, before we become familiar with our wild neighbors, I go out to take a photograph of Cathy and Meg swimming in the river. Unlike her father, Meg took to the water early, encouraged by her longtime baby-sitter, from New Zealand, whose citizens seem to be natural-born swimmers, as was my island-born mother. Cathy hollers ashore: "There's an odd bird. It makes a song like *'She, she.'*"

"It's a sharp-tailed sparrow," I tell her, knowing the song she is imitating and having already identified these peachy-cheeked sparrows as they perched on the marsh's now-tall grasses.

Throughout the month of June, I wait for this late-arriving bird, whose song is as unprepossessing as the willet's is bold. These two species are the only true marsh nesters at this northerly latitude. I feel privileged that a pair of the sharp-tails has chosen the Old Marsh as a nesting ground. Like the willets, these marsh nesters are relatively rare, having suffered a loss of habitat due to dyking, draining, and infilling of salt marshes.

The sharp-tail announces its return with its winsome call. I usually see and hear the first one near the *aboiteau*. The song of the sharp-tail is hard to describe: it is an inelegant, squishy sound akin to that of water in a rubber boot, a squeegee, or perhaps a tenor racked by laryngitis. "It's sort of a cool song," Meg says, as if to compensate for the bird's innate lack of musical talent, as well as her father's unaccountable delight in it.

This bird is an introvert, as secretive as the willet is showy. I hear it more often than see it. Sometimes it perches on the *Spartina pectinata* that graces the top of the dyke, but most times it tunnels through the tall grasses, where its nest is also hidden.

Sharp-tails build small, deep nests of soft grasses, attaching them to the stems of new grass so that their bottom rests close to the ground. I know the nest must be near the *aboiteau,* as that is where I see them briefly flutter up, then dive down to hide in the tall grasses. They have been compared with, and mistaken for, mice, as they tend to run along the ground rather than fly when getting from one place to another, feeding on insects, larvae, and sand fleas in the damp muds of the marsh bottom as they go.

Again, I have never found a sharp-tail's nest, and again I must refer to Harrison Lewis, who, that same summer of 1920, on June 12—two days before he finds the willet's nest at Cook's Beach—pedaled his bicycle several kilometers from Brook Farm to Bunker Island, at the southern end of Yarmouth Harbour, where he found "the occupied nest of a pair of Acadian Sharp-tailed Sparrows ... the first definitely identified nest of the species recorded from Nova Scotia." It was, he writes, "a neat, round cup of fine dead grass, with some horsehair in the lining." He found it on a low, grassy ridge, suspended on a mat of dead "eel-grass," which, he surmised, had been tossed up on the ridge by a storm. "The nest was not sunk on the ground at all," he emphasized. There were two partly feathered young (nearly ready to leave their nest) in their "snug home," and the dried body of a third lying on the front of the nest. From a safe distance, he watched the parents bring food to the two survivors for about an hour.

Lewis returned five days later, on June 17, to find the nest deserted and "thoroughly wet," having been flooded by the high spring tides driven by the new moon the day before. This leads him to speculate that the birds must have built the nest after the last new moon, on May 18, and as the intervening high tides accompanying the full moon, on June 1, would not have been as high, they would not have flooded the nest, which then would have contained eggs.

Lewis is properly intrigued by the nesting birds' apparent impeccable timing. "It would be interesting to know if this was a mere coincidence," he writes, "or if these birds, when nesting in salt marshes, take into account the variations in the rise and fall of the tides, and thus, indirectly, the phases of the moon!"

Over the years I have learned to expect the arrival of the nesting sharp-tails around the first full moon in June. Timing, it seems, *is* critical, for the male—the "singer"—must attract a mate, and the female must mate, build a nest, and hatch her young, between the highest tides that might flood the nest site. Like Lewis, I have come to believe that these birds do track the phases of the moon.

I LOVE THE ALACRITY of nature, its knowing, precise timing. Like the ancients, it seems, the creatures' calendar is run by the sun and the moon, the intensity of light and rhythm of the tides. But in some ways, this is as true for us, as marsh dwellers, as it is for them.

Mornings I often go down to the dock to sip my coffee. I hear the sharp-tail in the grasses across the river, shushing, keeping its low profile. I look into the waters, which are tannin rich from their drainage of inland bogs, but are clear near shore, and see little fishes darting this way and that.

As I'm sitting on the dock, listening to the morning birds and watching the little fishes, the tide is resting, or as we say in the East, "asking high." There is no motion either way, upriver or downriver. Suddenly, however, the tide turns, giving me the vertiginous sensation of being on a spinning planet. For a moment I am aware that I am not only part of the biosphere but also part of galactic space. The two—life on Earth and the mechanical forces of the universe—are intimately connected, the former deriving its impetus and sustaining energy from the latter. We are, through the rhythms of nature, reacquainted every day with the cosmological genesis, the Big Bang, that set everything in motion. For our family, living on a tidal river, the twice-daily comings and goings of the tide are constant reminders of the pull of the moon, the gravitational forces that drive our solar system and the ecosystem of our backyard.

On a lesser, but hardly less awe-inspiring, scale, we are connected to distant parts of the planet. During our second summer on the marsh this fact was brought forcefully home. On June 27, 1991, I wrote:

> It is utterly ominous outdoors. At noon there is the half light of dusk. The sky is vividly yellow. Smoke from forest fires in Quebec is drifting down on high altitude winds, obscuring the sun. Yet, on the ground, it is breathless, not a zephyr. A burnt smell lingers in the air. Is this how it is when they burn the rainforests of Brazil, an acrid reminder of doom on the wind? It brings home forcefully how closely linked events are on this globe washed by wind and tide.

Our daily lives beside the marsh and river are measured by a tidal clock. We swim, as my mother and I did, around the time of the high tide, as the tidal currents are least strong then. By late June the water has warmed enough to entice us to take the plunge. Just before high tide, Cathy and I float upriver and around the bend above our house, treading water, letting the flow of the tide propel us, as it does the moon jellyfish that drift passively, carried up the river from the strait by the strong incoming current.

The Tidnish is a so-called oxbow river that meanders back and forth, gaining sediment on one side, which, in its constant twisting and turning, it deposits on the far bank—robbing Peter to pay Paul. Its winding course, a slowly unraveling circle, seems to take the maximum amount of time and space to reach the sea. This gentleness is deceptive, however, as the tidal current is so strong that one can't swim against it.

We feel the warm water enfolding us. A few jellies drift along with us, pulsing like lacy parasols as they go, and above us an osprey and a bald eagle parry, vying for the few gaspereaux still running the river. Tree swallows dip around our heads to harvest an emerging hatch. A powerboat slows as it passes us, and the master, looking up at the circling raptors, quips: "They're looking for you."

We laugh and continue our dead drift. Soon the tide will turn, and like a pendulum, we will drift back downriver to our starting point.

7

THE HIDDEN MARSH

ALTHOUGH IT IS NOW high summer, the mature spartina rippling in the wind like a maritime wheatfield, much of the marsh life is hidden from my view as I work in my study. The flush of spring migrants, both fishes and birds, has passed through. The White Birch fox cubs have left the care of their mother and range freely in search of a new territory, so my sighting of one is rare and fleeting. Now that the den is abandoned I cross the river, pulling the canoe through the derelict *aboiteau* and beaching it in the drainage canal. As I tramp through the center of the marsh, *Spartina patens* caresses my bare feet, a familiar feeling I have always loved, silky and giving. Meg has dubbed this grass "mattress grass," which well describes its soothing effect. I am glad she has felt its caress as I did as a child. I remember, too, the harshness of its taller, coarser cousin, *Spartina alterniflora,* whose sharp leaves could inflict a cut, clean as paper, to a barefooted boy picking his way along the marsh edge at the mouth of the creek and swimming hole. As I pass the marsh pools, schools of mummichogs explode in all directions, as if someone has fired buckshot into the water.

The den is on high ground but as close to the marsh as possible without risk of being flooded by spring tides. The foxes have probably also chosen the site for its sandy soils, which are easy to dig and drain well. They have excavated an entrance under the alders where the cubs often shelter—the area I call the playpen. A second entrance, with its tailings of red sand, is higher up, 3 to 4.5 meters (10 to 15 feet) farther back in the woods. Standing on the roof of their modestly domed house, looking down, I don't see any tracks, even though it has been raining in recent days, telling me the foxes abandoned the den some time ago. The only sign of their occupancy is an unlucky rabbit's foot, a remnant of the cubs' tussle over the hare carcass earlier in the spring.

With nothing much more to see, I cross back over the marsh. A hummingbird buzzes by in the direction of the feeder as I work my way carefully along the dyke, hoping to find a sharp-tailed sparrow's nest. Again I fail in my nest-finding role, but I do discover on the river side of the dyke a small patch of samphire greens, which have colonized a bare patch of ground, and with it a few half shells of ribbed mussels, both true salt marsh species.

Of all the molluscs, the ribbed mussel is the best adapted to, and most characteristic of, the salt marsh. Although a similar color to the blue mussel of the rocky shore, the ribbed mussel's shell is not so smooth; it has the look of layered crinoline. The ribbed mussel is one tough customer, however, able to tolerate large swings in temperature, from $-22°$ to $38°C$ ($-8°$ to $100°F$), and to survive having three-quarters of its flesh fast-frozen. It can also tolerate widely varying salt concentrations.

Although the ribbed mussel grows best in small colonies along creeks and drainage canals, where it is flooded frequently, it can also survive for long periods out of water by "air-gaping," or breathing air directly, an ability marine molluscs do not possess. When submerged, it is a passive filter feeder, straining from the water whatever organic food the tide delivers. It produces a so-called pseudofeces, consisting of excess pieces of food stuck together by mucus, and it must grow up through this accumulating mound of by-product. This material is high in phosphates, which feed other organisms—mussels perform an important function in recycling nutrients in the marsh ecosystem. In midsummer, when temperatures rise to between $22°$ and $28°C$ ($72°$ and $82°F$) in the shallow waters of the strait, they produce their spawn, which become part of the rich planktonic soup drifting in and nourishing the estuary. At low tide, the mature mussels (inedible for humans) are preyed upon by raccoons on their nocturnal marsh raids.

The samphire greens (*Salicornia* sp.) are bushy little plants, only several centimeters high, that go by a variety of common names: samphire, an English corruption of the French St. Pierre, for the herb of St. Peter; crowfoot, for its shape; saltwort, because of its salty taste; and glasswort, because of its translucent, fleshy appearance when it is full of water. It has long been used as a pickle, or to add tang to salads, giving it yet another name, pickle plant. I pick a piece, and its salty but sour taste bites sharply on my tongue and at the back of my teeth as I board the canoe and paddle across the river.

FEW PLANTS AND ANIMALS can adapt to the harsh conditions of a salt marsh, the constant flooding and drying cycles accompanying the ebb and flow of tides. The most stressful factor, however, is the fluctuating salt concentrations. Most land plants cannot cope with salt. But salt marsh grasses—the spartinas— have adapted magnificently. They are the marsh builders, catching and retaining soil imported on the tides, raising the level of the marsh incrementally, a few grains at a time. They are also the primary source of the great productivity of the salt marsh, providing a standing crop for herbivores and a habitat for a myriad of microscopic creatures, and exporting their biomass to the surrounding marine environment, where it is broken down and powers the food web. These evolutionary wonders are the very essence of a salt marsh. Without them, it could not exist.

On the Old Marsh, the spartinas are a triad. Lining the riverbank, the tidal creeks, and the drainage canals is the saltwater cordgrass *Spartina alterniflora,* which is flooded almost daily and reaches heights of 1.2 to 1.5 meters (4 to 5 feet). It is a coarse grass with large spear-shaped leaves. Growing atop the dyke is Prairie cordgrass, *Spartina pectinata.* It is mostly dry-footed, subject to the tides and salt only during extremely high spring tides or during storm surges. The majority of the marsh inside the dyke is carpeted with Meg's "mattress grass," or formally, the salt-meadow grass *Spartina patens,* and is flooded most days of the month, except during the neap tides. It is this grass that Sherman, like the other saltwater farmers before him, cut for fodder and bedding. Every fall, after haying, he would remove the clapper on the *aboiteau* to allow the tides to flood his hay field, since the seeds of *S. patens* require soaking in salt water to germinate. This time-honored practice is called tiding and has a secondary benefit of renewing the fertility of the soil, as each tide brings a dressing of natural fertilizer from the sea to the marsh. In this way the productivity of the salt marsh hay fields has been maintained for centuries, since the time of the Acadians, without need for manure or artificial fertilizers.

What all three of these grasses have in common—and what the thousands of land plants, which would otherwise dominate the salt marsh, do not—is an ability to cope with salt.

Maintaining a correct balance of salts and water within the living cell is critical to its function, indeed its survival. Water moves back and forth across the membrane that encases the cell by osmosis. The water contains dissolved materials, including salts. It is vital that the concentration of salts in the cell and in its environment be equal. If the cell contains more salt than its environment, water moves into the cell, inflating it; if less, water moves the other way, deflating the cell.

Because of this osmotic pressure gradient, when most plants are exposed to salt water, water flows out of their cells, causing them to wither and die. The salt marsh grasses cope with this deadly phenomenon by drawing salt water into their cells and selectively concentrating salts there (principally sodium chloride, or sea salt), in an attempt to equalize the osmotic pressure on either side of the membrane. Too much salt within their cells, however, would also kill the salt marsh grasses, essentially blowing them apart as more and more water flowed into the cells. To rid themselves of excess salt, water is drawn in through the root membranes, and the leaves of the spartinas are furnished with specialized glands that secrete the excess salts in a very concentrated solution through pores on the leaf surface. Water in this solution evaporates under the sun, leaving behind salt crystals, which sparkle in the light. This hidden, complicated process not only explains the ability of the spartinas to survive and thrive on the marsh but also accounts for the silvery sheen that the grasses sometimes give off as they bend and wave in the summer winds.

Spartinas are not the only plants that have evolved to cope with the salt environment of the marsh, but they are so good at it that they crowd out most other vegetation. Their dominance is so complete as to give the illusion that nothing else grows there. This, of course, is not true. Given the stresses of this tidal environment, the diversity of plants growing on and around the marsh is quite impressive, as I learn when I join my friend Bill, the lawyer-botanist, for an afternoon of "botanizing" on the Old Marsh. "The salt marsh is floristically simple but ecologically complex," says Bill as we set out from the dock, paddling across the river to the *aboiteau.*

Like all stressful environments—and the salt marsh is among the most stressful—the marsh is characterized by relatively low diversity but very high productivity among those few plants that can cope. On the salt marsh, wetness and salinity are the prime factors limiting diversity, along with the mechanical friction of the daily coming and going of the tides and the seasonal jugger-naut of ice.

"'Plants grow where they can, not where they want,'" says Bill, quoting the great nineteenth-century botanist Sir Joseph Dalton Hooker, author of the *Genera Plantarum* (describing some 97,000 species of plants) and one of the staunchest defenders of the theory of natural selection proposed by his friend Charles Darwin. "Plants don't have a will, like us."

I suspect that Bill and I would have been happier living in the nineteenth century, in the infancy of modern science, when the distinction between amateur and professional was blur-red. Then, what the naked eye or the simple light microscope could see was enough to define a species. Today that definition can only be determined by counting chromosomes, by probing the hidden structure of protein pairings that make up the organism's DNA. This high-tech exploration of the molecule of life, a kind of chemical jungle, is no less inspired or fraught with intellectual twists and turns than the adventurous voyages of discovery of a century ago, but it lacks the sensuality of being in the field—of seeing, feeling, or even tasting a species where it lives.

Bill is a learned man in the Renaissance sense. He will patiently explain the historical roots of the notary public (if you are naïve enough to ask), quote liberally from Shakespeare, and delight in stumping me, a poet, with a question like, "Who first recognized Odysseus when he returned to Ithaca?" The answer—not his faithful wife, Penelope, as I said, but his dog, Argos.

It is not only his catholic learnedness that recommends him as a friend but his eccentricities, both cultivated and natural. He captains the most beautiful boat on the river, an antique lobster boat with an inboard make-and-break engine, or "one lunger." It is legendary among all river dwellers. I can hear it cough and throb into life when Bill kicks the flywheel at the dock, 2 kilometers (a mile or so) downstream, and its incessant *thwack, thwack, thwack*—a rhythmic series of violent backfires as gas ignites in its single piston—as he makes his way upriver. As the sound becomes louder, I pour a couple of drams of Scotch, for, among his other virtues, Bill is a man of refined taste. I meet him at the dock where, like old salts, we indulge in a gam before he proceeds to his newly built home upriver.

In mid-July, when much of the marsh vegetation is at its peak, Cathy and I follow Bill and his wife, Sylvia, as they do a transect across and around the marsh, identifying the plants as we go by both their scientific Latin names and their common names. I took a single course in general botany at university, and plants have never been my strong suit as a naturalist. In contrast, for more than a decade Bill spent his weekends in company with a salt marsh specialist at nearby Mount Allison University and has coauthored scientific papers on the marsh flora of the Chignecto region. I could have no better, nor more amiable, guide to the botanical residents of the salt marsh, hitherto unknown to me.

The Old Marsh does display a greater diversity of plants than the marsh of my childhood, in part because the former was dyked and a generation ago was still being hayed; also, it is a high marsh, unlike the low marsh that surrounds the Chebogue River, where the tidal range is twice what it is along the Northumberland Strait. On the Chebogue four-fifths of the marsh was low marsh, flooded daily, and therefore dominated by *Spartina alterniflora*.

On the Old Marsh, *S. alterniflora* grows only along the riverbank and drainage canals and around the marsh pools, where it is wetted by the tide daily. As we make our way through the *S. patens* of the middle of the marsh, Meg's "mattress grass," Bill stops to examine and identify patches of other salt-tolerant plants that have insinuated themselves among the dominant spartinas. In the classic *Life and Death of the Salt Marsh,* John and Mildred Teal write: "They [*Spartina* sp.] rule the marsh through sheer tonnage produced and space occupied. The rest of the marsh plants are like so many relatives attached to a strong household, of some importance in the social setup but not in the chain of command." It is these interlopers that most interest me on this occasion.

There are the usual suspects: black grass (*Juncus gerardi*), orach (*Atriplex* sp.), and arrow grass (*Triglochin maritima*). Black grass pokes its head above the marsh hay and possesses a small lilylike flower (it belongs to the lily family). The scaly blossom hardly looks like a flower, however, and the leaves are spikes, bristling like quills among the soft *S. patens.* I recognize each of these plants by sight but for the first time identify them by name. Like the spartinas, they are all halophytes, literally, "salt lovers."

"Sylvia, the book," Bill shouts. The book in question is *The Flora of Nova Scotia* by A.E. Roland. Sylvia cheerfully brings "the book." Bill's command might be mistaken for male chauvinism if one didn't know the couple better. Theirs is a lifelong romance fueled by a mutual interest in the outdoors and history and a lively sense of humor. A nurse by training and a Tidnish girl, Sylvia is also a seasoned amateur archeologist who has dug in Italy and Greece.

We kneel to first identify and then admire a seashore buttercup (*Ranunculus cymbalaria*) in bloom. It is a beautiful little flower, displaying five yellow petals, and one of the flowering plants one expects to find on the salt marsh—though, generally, flowering plants are rare. A little farther on we come across another diminutive yellow bloom belonging to *Potentilla anserina*, or silverweed, so called for the silvery "hairs" under its sawtoothed leaves.

Later, when Bill sends me the floral list from our botanizing trip around the Old Marsh, he encloses a *Scientific American* article titled "The Loves of the Plants," containing this baroque quote from the master botanist of all time, Carl Linnaeus:

> *The flowers' leaves . . . serve as bridal beds which the Creator has so gloriously arranged, adorned with such noble bed curtains, and perfumed with so many soft scents that the bridegroom with his bride might there celebrate their nuptials with so much the greater solemnity. When now the bed is so prepared, it is time for the bridegroom to embrace his beloved bride and offer her his gifts . . .*

Tiny blooms of the modest salt-loving flowers bedded among the marsh grasses bring a similar kind of rapturous pleasure to Bill and Sylvia.

There are other hidden delights to be found, including wild morning glory and sea lavender. The latter is not yet in bloom, but when it does blossom it may be picked; its petite lavender flowers will make a beautiful bouquet, lasting months. At the high tide mark, Bill identifies Scotch lovage, or seaside celery, a species that in northern marshes marks the upper limit of the salt marsh. In the southeast corner of the marsh is a stand of cattails (*Typha angustifolia*, or narrow-leafed cattail). This species bears both flowering parts on its rangy stem, the smaller male flower above the fuller female part. Unlike its freshwater cousin the broadleaf cattail, a denizen of bogs and ditches, it prefers the slightly saline waters of the upper salt marsh.

Having crossed the marsh, we walk along the tree line, where Bill identifies forty-odd trees, bushes, and plants that make up my jagged horizon and the Oriental screen of blossoms that decorate the marsh in May, including rhodora, a wild rhododendron that splashes the landscape with its rose-purple blooms, and chokecherry, with its delicate blush of pink blossoms. The bushes and shrubs, like the bayberry, while not salt loving are at least salt resistant and can survive the odd soaking that very high tides and storm surges occasionally deliver.

At the far northeast corner of the Old Marsh, Sylvia, exercising her archeological instincts, discovers a few old foundation stones, the scanty remains of some long-departed river dweller.

The first inhabitants of the region were the Mi'kmaq, who had an encampment at Tidnish Head, near what is now Jackson Point, where they also buried their dead. The first European settler was one Charles Chappell, a Loyalist of French descent whose surname had been anglicized from la Chappelle. His Huguenot ancestors had been driven from France by the St. Bartholomew's Day Massacre in 1572 and found refuge in England, to which they remained loyal two centuries after emigrating to the New World.

Charles's parents had arrived in Baie Verte in 1763, and in 1800 Charles rowed across the bay and up the Tidnish River, blazed his way through thick forests of hemlock, and on a hill overlooking the river built himself a log cabin. He received a land grant of some 120 hectares (300 acres), which included all the land at the mouth of river. Charles and his wife, Eleanor Thompson, had twelve children, and today, according to local history, through intermarriages, "Chappell blood [is] in the veins of a good number of present-day residents with other names," including my neighbor Sherman Davidson, a great-great-grandchild of the first settler.

Charles is said to have worn his hair in shoulder-length curls and to have been friends with the local Mi'kmaq chief, with whom he often hunted geese and ducks along the shore. Moose and caribou—the latter extirpated from Nova Scotia in 1900—were plentiful, as were herring, smelts, and other fish in the bay and the river, the staples of these early colonists.

The forest was the economic mainstay of the growing community, and water-powered mills sprang up along the feeder streams of the Tidnish River, which served for log drives. During the last days of the nineteenth century, and the opening ones of the twentieth century, several million board feet of lumber was exported annually to Europe and Newfoundland on barques. As many as twenty-nine Norwegian-registered sailing vessels were anchored in the bay at one time for this purpose. Small, oceangoing schooners were built at a place called the Shipyard, upriver from where we now live, and hauled on the ice by horse and oxen to the bay, where they were outfitted with masts for the coastal trade to the Caribbean and the eastern seaboard. The biggest economic boon to the area, however, was the building of Ketchum's ship railway, which attracted hundreds of Italian laborers. Hotels, stores, and warehouses sprang up to service the workforce before the great project was abandoned in 1891.

Around the same time, an important industry was established on the banks of the river where our house and that of our neighbors Charles and Doris Bugley now stand. The Chappell Brothers' woodworking plant turned out furniture, doors, and windows, as well as sawing lumber. Nothing remains of the factory, mill, or large cookhouse that once stood here. However, for a few hundred meters along the riverbank, slabs from the sawed logs are buried in the marsh mud. In many places they stick out, like piles of jackstraws. If it weren't for them, the riverbank would have eroded away long ago—and our house would not be here.

Little else remains to suggest the rich history of this place to the casual passerby. A notable exception is the beautiful stone culvert, built by British stonemasons to divert the river as part of the design of the ship railway, that is still visible to motorists as they cross the bridge 2 kilometers (a mile or so) down the river from our house. A century ago, the British bankers foreclosed on Ketchum, the Italian laborers filtered away, the herring and smelts, once exported abroad, largely disappeared from the bay and river, and a fire swept through the Tyndall Woods, destroying much of the forest capital and people's livelihoods. The Chappell Brothers' plant closed in 1912. It is a story repeated in small communities throughout Maritime Canada, of a brief golden Age of Shipping, followed by a precipitous and lasting economic decline. Local men like Sherman kept a few milk cows but went to work in town, and eventually even the dykes were abandoned to the tides and the marshes reverted to the sea.

We return to the canoe atop the dyke, noting along the way that there are four *aboiteaux,* all derelict like the one (the largest) across from our house. On the dyke top, there are some tall, coarse plants, curled dock (*Rumex crispus*) and knotweed (*Polygonum* sp.), both weeds introduced from Europe—green reminders that the colonial history of North America included not only a peopling of the continent with immigrants but an introduction of exotic flora, not always to good effect.

ATLANTIC MARSHES have formed over the several thousand years that sea level has been rising since the retreat of the glaciers. If you dug deep enough, you would find layers of peat from previous marshes that grew, were inundated, and then grew again, one on top of another, in layer-cake fashion.

I remember my father saying to me when I was a boy: "There are cedars buried under the marsh and there are no cedars anywhere around here now." This cryptic observation has resonated with me ever since. Rare in Nova Scotia, a few cedars do exist around swamps, lakes, and springs in the interior part of southwestern Nova Scotia, I have read. But Dad was right: there are none along the coast.

Why do I remember such a trivial thing, spoken to me nearly a half century ago? The notion of something buried, to be dug up and discovered, certainly appeals to a youthful imagination. But the memory tells me more—even then I was intrigued by natural history, by the dynamics of a natural order that could grow a forest, drown it, and begin again. Only later, in my midtwenties, did I realize just how intensely interested I was in such things, a passion that lay dormant, hidden from myself, for many years. By then my father was dead, at age sixty-three.

He was an extraordinarily well-read man with a special interest in history. My lasting image is of him in his easy chair, after a day's hard labor, glancing up momentarily from a book before immersing himself again in his self-education. His wedding day picture shows him crammed into a suit that he has probably not worn in years. The button pulls at his expanded girth; his heavy hands hang awkwardly from the too-short sleeves. He looks unflinchingly at the camera through rimless, hexagonal bifocals. It is an intelligent face, even wise. In later years, he joked that he looked like "a professor out of work," an uncannily accurate description of his intellectual character and his lot in life. A bookish man, he spent his life laboring and bequeathed to his sons this frank advice: "The day you put on overalls, you might as well forget it." His daily ritual was to doff his overalls on getting home and immediately pick up his book.

I credit his charge for the richness of my own intellectual life, which has straddled literature and the natural sciences. His innate curiosity is seeded in me and, by dint of his labor, has had an opportunity to come to fruition—an opportunity time and circumstance did not grant him.

I admonish myself now for not asking to be shown this buried forest when I had the chance—but then I was only a boy, and like all youth, believed I and those I loved would live forever. I tell myself that we might well have tramped the marsh together to the site and shared our delight in this natural artifact that reveals much about the evolution of salt marshes.

The Nova Scotian geologist Sir William Dawson was the first scientist to describe such a "submarine forest," in a paper he presented to the London Geological Society on January 3, 1855. Some 326 paces from the edge of the marsh, at the head of the Cumberland Basin, near Amherst, he found "erect stumps and many prostrate trunks of trees ... scattered as in an open forest." The trees of this ancient forest, he determined, were typical dry upland species, pine and beech. The largest pine was about .75 of a meter (2½ feet) in diameter and exhibited about two hundred growth rings. He noted that other submerged forests had been found elsewhere around the shores of the Bay of Fundy and "uncovered in digging ditches in the marsh."

The marsh also contains the cultural history of the region. Two decades ago, not far from where Dawson made his find, near the Acadian-built Fort Beausejour, archeologists uncovered a hexagonal, slate "bayonet." Its ornateness suggests that it probably was a burial talisman and belongs to the Maritime Archaic tradition, dating to four thousand years ago. The mysterious people of this time depended upon marine resources for survival—in particular, marine mammals, such as porpoises. It was just at this time that the great Fundy tides and, as a result, salt marshes were forming at the head of the bay. The tides have subsequently destroyed much of the archeological record as they have eaten away at the shoreline, and it is something of a miracle that this exquisite artifact ever came to light to speak of the resourcefulness and the spiritual richness of this vanished culture.

The marsh muds, however, contain the whole history of the Acadian peoples who dyked the salt marshes, built thriving agricultural communities on these dyke lands, and then became victims of a colonial war when they were expelled from their homeland in 1755—a diaspora that scattered some Acadians to the American colonies, especially Louisiana, repatriated others to France, and exiled some as far away as the Falkland Islands. Others, including many in southwestern Nova Scotia, remained, helped to survive by their indigenous neighbors, the Mi'kmaq, who had always had better relations with the French than with the English.

WHEN THE ONE-ROOM country schoolhouses closed in the 1950s and were consolidated into regional schools, Acadian children from across the Chebogue River became my playground friends, kids with family names like Surette, Saulnier, d'Entremont, and Doucet. In the winter before I went to school, in 1955, one of these children disappeared. His anglophone name was Howard James Newell. Although I never knew him, he became a ghostly playmate, a tragic presence accompanying me on my forays into the marsh.

Howard Newell of Little River Harbour was six years old (a year older than me) when he mysteriously disappeared. He had been playing with his cousins and was last seen heading home. When he didn't arrive for supper, a frantic hunt was initiated. For two weeks hundreds of local people and police searched for him in vain. In the end he was presumed drowned.

One theory—the one I remember hearing—was that he had stepped into a marsh sinkhole that swallowed up his small body. I had been warned of these sinkholes, the size of a small boy's torso, and feared them. Howard's death became a cautionary tale. I liked to wander—on the marsh, up the brook, and through the back fields—but now the realization gripped me that I might literally disappear into the landscape. I thought of him often, especially as I picked my way through the marsh, eyes on the ground for just such a man trap, a trapdoor to oblivion. When the wind rippled through the grasses, I listened for a small voice, my marsh doppelgänger hailing and warning me.

As I think of it now, the theory of his drowning seems unlikely. Such sinkholes might well give you a good soaking, but they were not bottomless. Even if a small boy fell into one and did drown, his body would float up; he would not disappear forever into the marsh muds.

July

Forty years later, another theory emerged, one kept alive by rumor but long repressed by communal fear. The boy, walking home, had been struck by drunk drivers from a nearby community. Later they had destroyed the evidence on a pyre of car tires.

The case remains unsolved. The father, Harold Newell (now deceased), never believed his son had drowned on the marsh or in the Little River. He scoured the marsh and the approaches to the river. It was January when his son disappeared, and "there was ice as thin as paper laying all around, everywhere he could have got to the water," he told *The Yarmouth Vanguard* in 1995, forty years after his son's disappearance. "I went all around it and there were places where crows had laid down and broken the ice. There was no way that anything that weighed more than two pounds could get through that ice, you know, to water without leaving tracks. There was no way."

When I read this, I thought about how well this man knew the land, how precise his forensics were, seeing where the crows had taken their rest, and how little time had repaired his loss, the body prints of those black birds still clear in his mind as he searched for a trace of his son. I remembered my imaginary playmate and how he haunted the marsh of my childhood. He still does haunt my imagination, the memory of his survivors, and if the rumor is true, surely the consciences of the guilty.

JULY IS THE FULCRUM of the marsh year. The grasses have reached their maximum height and lushness. Soon this vegetative stage, this urge to growth, will slow and stop—unlike our own insatiable appetite—and the year will tip inexorably toward harvest and decay and, ultimately, dormancy and renewal.

It all seems to happen too quickly.

For a time, a state of suspension prevails over this ripest month. Animals are still active, but less so. Osprey continue to search the shallows for gaspereaux returning from their spawning grounds in the muddy shallows upriver or, spent by procreation, drifting dead. A lone blue heron frequents the river at low tide. An immature eagle drops in to loaf on a driftwood perch fetched up on the dyke. An occasional deer appears to crop the tall grasses. Riding on the blustery winds that buffet the marsh hay, tree swallows pluck the profligate salt marsh mosquitoes out of the air. A harrier glides over the marsh meadows on its stiff, barely beating wings. The quavering of a loon echoes from downriver, a young, unwary muskrat swims along the shoreline, and a flock of sandpipers flies low over the marsh, leaving behind a trail of little songs.

By midmonth, the first greater yellowlegs return to the marsh. They are the harsh heralds of a turning season. These northern breeding shorebirds are like a global barometer, an early warning system. Their appearance reminds me that there have been north winds lately, a subtle cooling of the nights. Now I know the Arctic summer is drawing to a close.

The nickname of these tall, stately shorebirds is "tattler." They are constantly raising the alarm—*keek, keek, keek,* ear-splitting notes—as a female marsh hawk drifts low over her hunting ground. They are the first of the northern breeding birds to arrive and the last to leave, lingering until the first skim of ice forms on the marsh pools.

Although some nights the air is already taking on a fallish tinge, the water holds its heat, warmed each day as it moves over the sun-drenched mudflats. Schools of minnows mingle in the shallows, some so small they are translucent, like neon bulbs flashing an electric green in the submarine murk. Perhaps these

July

are the gaspereau fingerlings making their leisurely way out to sea. And legions of jellies are floating with the tide, including ginger-colored lion's mane and red jellies, from the size of poached eggs to the diameter of softballs.

Cathy and I drift on the tide with just our heads bobbing above the water. We must be mistaken for driftwood as a flock of peeps (small sandpipers) whizzes by our ears, dividing and re-forming as they maneuver by this obstruction. It is an oddly satisfying sensation, for a moment to be inanimate, an indifferent object in the landscape. It is a curious phenomenon for another reason, as I discover when I dry off and go inside to check the calendar—July 19. A biologist friend of mine, who studies shorebirds, has told me that the semipalmated sandpipers arrive in the Bay of Fundy from their northern breeding grounds "on or about July 18th"—and here they are, precise as clockwork.

Living in one place for more than a decade, tracking its comings and goings, has taught me that the turning of the seasons with the patterns that accompany it, especially the appearance and disappearance of certain species, are like the finely tooled workings—the escapement—of a pocket watch. It is an apt, if somewhat dog-eared, metaphor, but birds, all creatures, can tell time, it seems.

The arrival of one species sometimes signals the departure of another, though this changing of the guard is not carried out with military precision. Such is the case with the willets and the yellowlegs.

The willet young have fledged, and I look out one morning to see six willets—a wonder of willets—perched on a driftwood snag, all in a row. The young add their pitched cries to the summer symphony. Soon, however, the willet choir will fall silent and be replaced by the hardly less strident chorus of the yellowlegs. It is as if there is not enough space, enough air, to accommodate the competing arias of these brassy shorebirds.

JULY BRINGS a surprise visitor to the river, like us, enjoying a free ride on the tide. The soft-eyed, glistening head of a female harbor seal pops up in front of us as Cathy and I sit in our lawn chairs by the riverside one evening. She sticks her head and shoulders out, regards us nonchalantly and dives, resurfacing closer this time, next to the dock, beckoning to us, it seems. Just then we see a father and son canoeing down the river. We gesture toward the seal, miming our delight, and they nod back knowingly. The seal dives and disappears as they paddle ashore. They tell us she has followed them upriver, all the way from the bridge, appearing beside them at intervals along the way and regarding them with that curiously beguiling expression that seems to be a permanent feature of seal physiognomy.

Whenever I observe or hear of seals behaving in this familiar way, I cannot help but think of the selkie legend. *Selkie* is the Orcadian dialect word for "seal." In the eighth century, when the Norse settled the Orkney Islands, off the northern tip of Scotland, they renamed the islands Orkneyjar, or the Seal Islands. The selkie legend, of seals assuming human form out of water and breeding with men and women, seems to have a much older pedigree, perhaps dating to the prehistoric Picts, who left petroglyphs of seals on the islands. The selkie tales spread up and down the north and west coasts of Scotland but were not written down until the eighteenth century. Some portrayed these shape-shifters as fallen angels; others thought that the selkie-folk were human beings cursed to assume the form of seals for misdemeanors in past lives. The popular (and less Puritan) notion among Orkney fisherfolk was that selkies were the souls of the drowned. The common element in all selkie folk tales is that seals cast off their skins to assume human form onshore and must reclaim them to return to the sea. Often the selkie took the form of a beautiful woman, and if a young man wanted to make her his bride, he had to steal and hide her seal skin. Both selkie-men and selkie-women were renowned for their seductive charms and were apparently fertile, producing children who had webbed feet as a mark of their origin. My own mother, born on a stony island off the tip of southwestern Nova Scotia to fisherfolk, has webbed toes.

This animal had a particularly strong feminine air about her. I wondered, where was the man's wife and the boy's mother? Who was this seal? But her secret thoughts were hidden from me. In the end, I could only say this seal seemed as interested in human affairs as I am in the workings of the wild.

8

TWIN REALMS

DURING the cricket-enchanted days of August I often sit on the dock. Emerald-colored dragonflies buzz from the tall grasses, their fairy wings clattering against the dry stalks as they make their predatory raids on other flying insects, grasping them in their basketlike legs.

There are about fifty insects—grasshoppers, crickets, and beetles—common to the salt marsh. Insects are well adapted to the changeable marsh conditions, since their hard exterior skeletons (exoskeletons) lock out water as well as salt. When the tide is out, they move freely about the marsh, and when the tide returns, many climb up the grasses to avoid getting wet or drowning. Many large insects are equipped to avoid drowning, even when covered by water for short periods. They can breathe air through tiny tubes and passages that are waterproofed and sometimes contain valves to prevent them from ingesting water. Even when the tubes are open, their waterproofing prevents wetting of the walls. And as a last resort, many submerged insects can go without oxygen until the tide recedes.

Looking down into the water from the dock, I see the grasses—spartinas—bending under the force of the retreating tide. Since childhood I have loved these submarine plants, alive with the energy of the tide, waving back at me. The unoriginal thought, "there's another world down there," recurs to me.

I was in my first years of school when I brought home from the library Charles Kingsley's *The Water Babies*. I curled up on the daybed in the farmhouse kitchen, next to the wood stove, to consume this children's classic. I could read a little, but the ornate Victorian prose of this nineteenth-century theologian-naturalist was extremely tiring to decipher and I soon resorted to merely looking at the drawings by Jessie Wilcox Smith: the fishes, dragonflies, crabs, turtles, lobsters, and jellies, the fearsome otter, and a large eel coiling around the boy's legs.

I was fascinated by the water babies, and by that I mean I was both attracted to and repelled by them. First I was attracted to the water babies because they were naked, though that fact also made me feel uneasy—that in a book nakedness should be depicted at all. I was repelled, however, not by their nakedness but by the notion that these babies lived and breathed underwater. The protagonist Tom, a little boy like myself, had drowned, like the boy across the marsh in Little River. Kingsley had rescued his hero, however, by having the fairies turn Tom into a water baby:

> *Tom, when he woke ... found himself swimming about in the stream, being about four inches, or—that I may be accurate—*

3.87902 inches long, and having round the parotid region of his
fauces a set of external gills (I hope you understand all the big
words) just like those of a sucking eft . . .

I'm afraid I didn't understand all the big words, but I did understand, somehow, that Tom had become a submarine creature,
capable of breathing underwater. Kingsley goes on to argue, in
terms a boy could not understand, how water babies just might
exist: "You must not say that this cannot be, or that this is contrary to nature. You do not know what nature is, or what she can
do; and nobody knows . . . " Not even Mr. Darwin, he claims,
though I'm sure I did not then know who Darwin was.

Kingsley's tale frightened, more than enlightened, me at the
time, afraid as I was of drowning. But his story, its lesson of
the seemingly infinite possibilities for adaptation and survival,
seems more plausible the more one learns of nature's variabil-
ity—something that Mr. Darwin understood very well and that
I have come to appreciate firsthand.

The salt marsh grasses, I now think, are like those water babies, inhabiting two realms, one in water and one in air, as they
are alternately covered and uncovered by the flooding and ebbing
tides. Humans also have a dual existence, one in solitude, which
seems submarine, and one in society, which is more aerial. And
the animals of the salt marsh, such as the ribbed mussel, can adapt
to being on dry land at one moment and underwater the next.

While sitting on the dock, I idly search the dry tops of the
Spartina alterniflora for a salt marsh snail (*Melampus* sp.) and am
surprised to find one. What an elegant little creature it is, tinier
than a newborn's fingernail and, in its spiraling architecture, as
beautiful as a miniature Etruscan vase. Like the grasses, it has
evolved an ingenious lifestyle to cope with the wetting and drying cycles of the salt marsh environment.

August

During low tide, the snail stays in the moist areas at the base of the grasses, which shade it from the hot sun. Since it has no operculum (a horny door marine snails possess to close the shell), it must seek damp places to avoid drying out. When the tide floods in, however, it is forced to climb the grass stalks, since it is a so-called pulmonate snail, furnished with a lung to breathe air. If by accident it is flooded, it can survive for an hour with its last breath while the tide drops away.

Its most remarkable adaptive mechanism is an internal alarm clock that anticipates the timing of the flood tide. Every twelve hours the alarm goes off, triggering the snail to begin climbing the grasses to avoid being drowned. How this tidal clock is set is still unknown.

Melampus has a second internal clock, which dictates the breeding cycle. Unlike other pulmonate snails, it begins life as a larva rather than a small snail hatched from an egg. The larva travels on the tides for a few weeks until it fetches up on a suitable portion of marsh, when it transforms into the snail form, replete with shell.

Each individual is a hermaphrodite, both male and female. It is unable to fertilize itself, however, and so must meet others of its own kind to complete the breeding cycle. A combination of warming waters and lengthening days triggers breeding. Shortly after the twice-monthly highest tides, these snails congregate in masses on the spartina stems, where they breed and lay their gelatinous masses of eggs.

This remarkable behavior is so hardwired that even if they are removed to a laboratory, they will continue to gather into breeding groups according to their native marsh's cycle of tides. It appears that this second, internal, breeding clock runs on a twenty-four-hour schedule, and when it is in phase with the tidal clock, the snails know that two weeks between spring tides has passed and it is again time to reproduce.

MUMMICHOGS ARE also highly attuned to the fluctuating tidal conditions of the salt marsh.

In the marsh pools, the number of minnows has been burgeoning since early June, when the mummichogs begin their spawning. "Mummichog" is of Indian derivation, meaning "going in crowds," and by August the marsh pools are indeed crowded with these chunky minnows, which are fast food for the returning herons, bitterns, and yellowlegs, as well as the fledgling kingfishers practicing their highwire art.

Like the other full-time residents of the salt marsh, this humble minnow—the most important food species in the salt marsh—is wonderfully adapted to the stresses of wetting and drying that come with the salt marsh territory.

Spawning appears temperature dependent, with the greatest peaks occurring at the beginning and the end of the summer, when the days are shorter and temperatures lower. As they prepare to spawn, males undergo color changes, the muddy green body becoming black on the back, steel blue on the sides, and yellow on the belly. They also become particularly cantankerous, the more brightly plumed among them driving away their paler competitors. To telegraph her readiness, the female with ripe eggs flashes her white belly, and the courtship begins with the male swimming below and slightly behind the female. During spawning the male clasps the female so that their ventral fins lock together, and he pushes her against the marsh pool bottom or side, whereupon she assumes an S-shape. The fish vibrate together, releasing eggs and sperm.

For all its abruptness, the timing of this act and the place-ment of the eggs is an object lesson in elegant planning. Spawn-ing takes place around the highest tides of the month, coinciding with the new and full moons, and usually at night, as that is when the higher of the two daily tides occurs. The fertilized eggs are sometimes deposited in pits in the mud, under mats of filamentous algae, in empty ribbed mussel shells, or on the inner leaves of *Spartina alterniflora*, all of which afford some protection from predation and dessication. In instances where the eggs are secured to a stalk of marsh grass, it is at a level just below where the highest spring tides reach. These eggs may be wetted but are not flooded by the neap tides, and there is evidence that they need exposure to the air, since they appear to develop more rapidly out of water. The next cycle of high tides, in two weeks, stimulates hatching, apparently triggered by a sudden decrease in oxygen accompanying the flooding of the eggs—a kind of in-duced labor. Experiments have shown that the air-incubated eggs begin hatching within seconds of being exposed to water. Embryos start to move within five minutes of exposure and hatch in fifteen to twenty minutes.

"WHAT IS THAT SOUND?" a perplexed friend asks one evening as we sit inside the River Room.

"Mosquitoes," I deadpan, though I can understand his confu-sion. The wing beats of the swarm sound like the hot tires of an eighteen-wheeler passing along the highway, or the distant roar of a jet overflying the Atlantic.

Specifically, the noisemaker is the saltmarsh mosquito, *Aedes sollicitans*. Like the mummichog, it is remarkably adapted to the wetting and drying cycles of the marsh.

This saltwater pest is easily distinguishable from its equally pesky freshwater cousin by the distinct white bands that mark its beak, legs, and abdomen and by another white band that runs lengthwise along its brown back. Regarding one drilling into my arm, I think that its striped body parts look like a convict's pajamas. And when the mosquitoes show up in swarms in the backyard, as they often do on summer nights, they are about as welcome as escaped jailbirds.

For the last century, saltmarsh mosquitoes have been subjected to a constant barrage of control measures: salt marshes have been drained and ditched, sprayed with pesticides, or doused with oil. Each of these drastic methods has often proven more effective in disturbing the ecology of the marsh than in controlling mosquitoes. The reason is simple: the saltmarsh mosquito is a flexible critter, capable of surviving under a wide variety of environmental conditions. For instance, it reproduces as effectively in fresh water as it does in water three times as salty as the oceans.

To thwart the breeding cycle, researchers have tried to figure out where and how mosquitoes reproduce. We now know that mosquito larvae don't do well in portions of the marsh that are flooded frequently, meaning that they proliferate in the upper marsh, dominated by *Spartina patens,* or salt-meadow hay. Here the females seek out debris or leaves, or simply moist ground, to deposit their eggs along or just above the water's edge. Although frequent flooding destroys or disperses the eggs, submergence of the eggs is necessary to induce hatching. A hatch is produced roughly every two weeks, at the time of the highest lunar tides.

The straight-bodied larvae then progress through several stages, all the while breathing air at the surface of the marsh pond. In nine days, they metamorphose into curved or crescent-shaped pupae and finally into winged adults, and one week later, this new generation is capable of laying eggs of its own.

The males survive exclusively by sucking plant juices. The females are the biting insects and require at least one blood meal to ripen their eggs. Males and females often swarm together, presumably to mate, but when mating takes place is not well documented. Saltmarsh mosquitoes swarm at dusk, a phenomenon I can attest to, for it is at this time that Cathy and I are driven from the backyard and the garden by this bloodthirsty sorority—clouds of them descending upon us from the marsh across the river.

I am bemused reading one biologist's charitable description of the flight of an egg-filled female mosquito (therefore one intent on extracting blood) as "slow, graceful, majestic," probably, he surmises, because of the heavily egg-laden abdomen.

As the range of tides increases in late summer, conditions improve for the production of these "majestic" creatures. On late-summer evenings, we take refuge in the River Room so that we might enjoy the dying of the light on the marsh without donating blood to its most unsympathetic residents. It does not stop them from trying, however, as they mass against the window screens, wanting in.

Although our response to *Aedes sollicitans* is avoidance, for other marsh residents mosquito swarms are a boon. The mummichogs' most important foodstuff is mosquito larvae. As they move through the mosquito-breeding marsh pools, or migrate through the grasses at high tide, they slurp a steady diet of these wrigglers. In fact, opening up the marshes to mummichogs has been shown to be the most effective, and least biologically destructive, method of mosquito control.

MOSQUITOES are not the only biting insects to mar the tranquility of the marsh, or the ones with the worst bite. That dubious distinction belongs to the horseflies, or green-heads (*Tabanus* sp.).

These brightly colored flies (it is their eyes that are green) have sizable jaws, or mandibles, the better to rip a chunk of flesh from their victims, which include all warm-blooded creatures. It is these pests that I remember best from childhood, when invariably one would tear a strip from my skinny frame while I was at the swimming hole or roaming the marsh.

The mosquitoes left less of an impression on me, perhaps because we swam mostly during the daytime tides, when they were less likely to swarm. But the salt marsh of my childhood was also not an ideal breeding ground for mosquitoes, as it was primarily low marsh that was flooded almost daily, as opposed to the high marsh that now borders our home. The persistent flooding discouraged mosquito breeding but was ideal for the breeding of green-heads, who like to lay their eggs on *Spartina alterniflora* leaves or stalks, which are submerged with each tide. Upon hatching, the large, fleshy white maggots plow through the muds, devouring everything in their path, including each other. Two years later, they metamorphose into the green-eyed, winged adults. They then mate, lay eggs, and die, all in the space of three weeks. It is only the larval-eating fishes and winged predators that give us marsh dwellers any respite from their rapacious ways.

AS I CANOE the river at dusk, I flush out a great blue heron fishing in the shallows. It flies off with a protesting croak, forced through its impressively long pipes. In the failing light, bats weave through the night air and swallows swoop in low, graceful lines over the water. And high up a pair of nighthawks—black against the darkening sky—feed in the updrafts, maneuvering on their stiff, white-striped wings like radio-controlled balsa toy planes and emitting a mechanical call like the beep of an antique roadster.

I notice this pattern again and again over the years—the swallows and bats work the lower echelons of the dusky swarms of mosquitoes, and the nighthawks prefer the higher strata of the swarms. It is as if these insect eaters had come to an agreement on how to divvy up the nightly banquet of flying insects. Although I have found no studies to confirm it, these predators appear to partition the sky into aerial niches, just as terrestrial species divide territory and resources on the ground.

In midmonth, we turn our gaze to the night skies for another kind of air show—the annual Perseid showers, meteors that rain through the atmosphere beginning on or about August 12. Mythologically, the meteors are the daughters of the Greek hero Perseus, who slew the serpent-coiffed Gorgon, Medusa, and rescued Andromeda from the sea monster. Like so many Greek heroes, he is fated to hang in the night sky, where his daughters tumble through space—like cosmic spawn—from his constellation.

Cathy and I sit out on a benignly mosquito-less night, watching the Perseids spark their tracery across the sky. Some are mere beads of white light trailing a long, if ephemeral, tail. Others, however, are like bulbs of blown glass, red-hot; still others are green as fireflies. And one comes apart in front of our eyes, fiery sparks flying as atmospheric friction tears it to pieces. Even such a sublime show of light cannot keep us up all night, however. Some stars will fall unseen.

In the morning when I wake and, as I always do, look at the marsh as my first act of the day, there is another streak of light—a small flock of sandpipers shooting downriver.

SHOREBIRDS LINGER LATE into the month, obsessively pecking at the mudflats, circling the marsh pools for a meal of invertebrates, in order to lay on enough fat for their imminent migration. At the head of the Bay of Fundy, hundreds of thousands form mesmerizing flocks to feed on the astronomical numbers of mud shrimp secreted in U-shaped burrows in the mudflats; the shrimp in turn are fed by the detritus flushed from the Tantramar Marsh. Here, on the Old Marsh and along the Northumberland Strait, the numbers of migrants are less impressive, though the marshes play the same critical role in fueling the food chain and the shorebirds' 4,000-kilometer (2,500-mile) flight over the open Atlantic to South America.

I hear a yellowlegs raising the alarm, and a merlin flashes by my field of vision in hot pursuit of a flock of peeps. This autumnal massing of shorebirds is critical to the success of both the merlin—a.k.a. pigeon hawk, a small, brown member of the falcon family—and its larger and much rarer relative, the peregrine falcon. They dive (called stooping, in raptors) through the large flocks, striking their prey with their extended claws and usually killing them in midair, in an explosion of feathers, as if the smaller bird had been shot.

Sometimes, despite their unsurpassed aerial prowess, these deadly falcons misfire. One day I get a call from a neighbor at the mouth of the river. An unidentified "hawk" has crashed into their picture window and now seems unable to fly away. As community naturalist and environmentalist, I also become de facto bird rescuer. On arrival, I discover the "hawk" is a falcon— a merlin.

Although the bird is grounded, its beak and claws deserve respect. I pursue it through the woods, where it runs away like a grouse or partridge—for a raptor, a most undignified gambit— maneuvering through the trees, keeping a safe distance between us, before I finally corner it against the house and capture it as gently as I can with a blanket. We bundle the pacified raptor (a chocolate-brown female) into the neighbor's van for transportation across the Tantramar Marsh to a bird rehabilitation center, where it is diagnosed as having suffered a concussion and released into the wild a day or two later.

IT IS HARVEST TIME on the old marsh.

The marsh is a biological factory par excellence. No agricultural crop, except rice and sugar cane, approaches the food production of the salt marsh. Tides ferry a perpetual supply of nutrients to the marsh, which the plants and animals recycle with breakneck rapidity. Bacteria in the muds produce a new generation every few hours, marine algae turn over in days, and even the grasses reproduce every six months. At best, a forest replicates itself every few decades. A small amount of this productivity is consumed on the stalk by herbivorous insects, such as grasshoppers and crickets, but most is exported on the tides to the estuary to feed crustaceans and molluscs and moves offshore to fertilize the fisheries. Within the marsh itself, energy flows every which way along the many strands of the food web, like game pieces in Snakes and Ladders.

Black ducks plow through greening marsh pools choked with pondweed. It is their favored fodder and also attracts blue- and green-winged teal as the long shadows of August advance. These smaller ducks, not seen since spring, tip up in the glancing light, their white rumps shining like chrome fenders. Blue herons return to the marsh in late summer, having dispatched their breeding and brooding duties on offshore islands in the strait. The bittern, looking as grumpy and disconsolate as ever, has also sought out the salt marsh, now that its young (O homely children) have been left to their own devices. The kingfishers that nest in the riverbank are fledged, and their calls, like the ratchet of a spooling fishing reel, announce that they are about to plunge for minnows schooling in the miniature underwater forests of the pondweed. Yellowlegs stalk through the pools on their tall, mustard-colored stilts, and least sand-pipers—the smallest of this dainty shorebird clan—whirl like wind-devils around the marsh. I pick them out from their slightly larger cousins, the semipalmated sandpipers, by the chocolate hue of their feathers and their rattlelike trill, as if they had a small pea stuck in their throat. A spotted fawn gambols through the shoulder-high strands of Lucius's Marsh. The grasses, raising their heads into the wind, are beginning to go to seed.

TODAY FARMERS begin harvesting their hay crop as early as June, when the fodder is greenest and richest in protein. In my father's time, small, mixed farmers could not afford silos to store this green first cut, and besides, to make such wet hay created a fire hazard, as it was likely to combust spontaneously in an open barn. And in southwestern Nova Scotia, the persistent summer fogs, created by tidal upwellings, always seemed to linger until midmorning and made for poor haymaking weather until the dog days of August.

Dad waited until then, when the hay, the timothy and fescue, went to seed, or "top," as he used to say. I remember haying time as a kind of festival. By then my father no longer kept horses; nor did he own a tractor. Neighbors came to help him bring in the hay. My mother brought sandwiches and cold drinks to the fields as the bare-chested men labored under the hot August sun. But she had also lent muscle and sweat to the task before the men arrived by making windrows with a large wooden rake (I remember it, broken and abandoned, on the barn floor when I was young) and turning it with a steel fork to dry. In my mind's eye, I see her: a young, strong woman like a figure in Jean-François Millet's *The Gleaners*.

Too young to be of much help, I waited for the wagon to be loaded, a mountain of loose hay forked above the side racks by the sun-weathered men who hoisted me atop the bulging load like a young rajah onto an elephant's back. There I proudly rode, rolling to and fro with the shifting weight. I might be taken down as we negotiated the gateway through the rock wall that divided the back pasture from the hay field, which, besides hay, sprouted healthy crops of daisies and buttercups, which colored the fields with pointillist splashes of white and yellow. Then it was aboard again for the final ride up to the barn, where the wagon was backed through the great doors between the mows.

The loading fork was a large, hinged claw mounted by block and tackle and run on rails down the center of the barn. It had an animal power—like a giant, airborne crab. It lurched forward, then was dropped and buried in the flanks of the load, the men kicking it into place to secure its purchase. My oldest brother, Greg, remembers when a horse was harnessed to pull the load up and along the central track and the fork was tripped, the hay collapsing into the mow in a swirling cloud of golden motes and chaff. (In my time the borrowed tractor or a car was hitched to hoist the load.) I watched at a safe distance, for it was at this stage that there was danger. The tines of the great fork might not hold; the mechanism to release the hay might not trip. I do not remember that any such disaster occurred, only that I was always warned to "stand clear."

We did not harvest any salt marsh hay, and it seemed that no one else along the Chebogue River had done so for a long time. But some of the weathered, raised platforms that held the marsh hay above the tide still stood on the marsh. They were known as staddles. The hay was stored there in the fall and only removed

when the marsh froze over, when a wagon could pass safely over
the spongy ground. Mounds of hay were still piled atop a few of
these venerable structures, a harvest that for whatever reason
had never been retrieved and was now slowly rotting. The image
of these staddles—legs planted firmly in the marsh and a high
back of hay—inspired Dad's colorful name for marsh hay: elephant grass.

BY THE THIRD WEEK of August, there are irrefutable signs that
autumn is nearly upon us.

One evening I look up to see a wedge of waterfowl. At first I
think they are black ducks because they are small, but they are
honking and are in a gooselike V-formation. Then it comes to
me: they are brant, a smaller cousin of Canada geese. They are
headed for the strait, where their prime food, eelgrass (*Zostera
marina*) grows luxuriantly in the shallow, warm waters. *Zostera* is
the only flowering plant in the north that can complete its life
cycle submerged in salt water, normally fatal to flowering
plants. But in the early 1930s, eelgrass beds were decimated all
along the eastern seaboard by a fungal pathogen known as the
wasting disease. Brant specialize in eating eelgrass, and as a result, their numbers collapsed.

The ubiquitous Harrison Lewis investigated the disappearance of the eelgrass in the Sept-Îles region, on the north shore of
the St. Lawrence River, along the brant's traditional migration
route to and from Ungava Bay. "In May and June, 1935," he
wrote, "I made two visits in search of eel grass ... but did not
find one living eel-grass plant."

The loss of the eelgrass meadows also resulted in a major decline in fisheries populations, including cod, shellfish, and scal-
lops. It appears that eelgrass beds, which are richly coated with
micro-algae, act as nurseries for various larval fish species.

Slowly the eelgrass beds have recovered and, with them, brant populations. Great mats of uprooted eelgrass move up and down the river with the tides throughout the summer, and in the fall local residents still collect windrows of this saltwater grass along the shore to bank their houses against the coming winter blasts.

My friend and neighbor Dick Beswick, who has a cottage on the shores of Baie Verte, has observed that the blue herons—upwards of fifty at any one time—prefer to feed in the eelgrass beds at midtide. Small fishes are abundant there, but Dick, an engineer, also believes that the beds act as natural weirs, corralling the fish and making it easier for the herons to harvest them—an idea that bears further investigation.

Although they prefer the shore, there is always one or more great blue herons fishing the river or marsh pools across from our house. The flooding tide seems to improve conditions for this great fisher, perhaps bringing more fish from the river and drainage canals into the marsh pools, or merely deepening them, allowing for improved stealth.

What stealth! I watch as a lone heron stands stock-still waiting for a school of minnows roiling the surface to come within striking distance. Water drips from his bill tip—the residue of a previous strike—but otherwise he does nothing to betray his presence. As the minnows come closer, he relaxes the S-scroll of his neck but does not uncoil it. Slight muscular twitches show his anxiousness, however. He raises his right leg, thinking to step forward, but abandons the idea. He stands, seemingly frozen by indecision, as the wary minnows swirl out of reach. Such patience—and frustration!

As the heron awaits his chance, a kingfisher falls from the sky, striking when the heron could not and underscoring the differences in strategy of these two consummate fishers—one a water-bound wader, the other an aerial diver—though both strike with lightning speed when the timing is right.

WEIGHTY CUMULONIMBUS CLOUDS billow up from the horizon, their underbellies darker than those of the popcorn-style clouds of a few weeks earlier. The monochromatic green of high summer is giving way to a richer, earthier palette. Russet hues begin to creep up the stalks of the *Spartina alterniflora*. The seaside goldenrod shake their gilded heads along the drainage canals and dyke, illuminating the marsh boundaries like gold-leaf lettering on a medieval manuscript. Daily, more blue-winged teal skid to a landing on the marsh pools. Their wing coverts flash, iridescent as a facet of labradorite in the strong August light. Resplendent in her rufous plumage, a female marsh hawk cants effortlessly over the dyke—stopping and starting with hardly a wing beat in between—raising the yellowlegs' obstreperous alarm. An immature bald eagle makes regular visits to the marsh and seems to cry disconsolately—perhaps not yet used to its solitary life out of the nest.

The number of black ducks and blue-winged teal enjoying the summer harvest of duckweed continues to grow throughout the month. In the mornings a silver sheen surrounds these dabbling ducks, their feeding creating mercurial circles in the marsh pools.

Fox kits, now fully grown, seek shade under the spruce at the marsh edge, making the ducks nervous and vigilant. Their wariness, though prudent, is probably unnecessary in the heat. Exertion on such a hot, humid day means an energetic loss, an equation the foxes appear to instinctively compute.

These dog days soon pass and activity picks up on the river and marsh, as shadows lengthen and the month advances toward the equinox.

August draws to a close with a crescendo. Green-winged teal now join the blue-winged teal in ever-greater numbers; yellowlegs, both greater and lesser, congregate on the little islands that dot the marsh pools. They, along with the blue herons and kingfishers, will linger a while longer to take advantage of the summer production of minnows. A muskrat emerges from the *aboiteau* to glean several stalks of spartina, which he carries in his mouth like a sheath of golden wheat.

9

A TIME OF TURMOIL

AS THE DAYS of summer wind down, great blue herons congregate on the Old Marsh, each staking its own claim. A blue heron cruises by to police his territory and finds another feeding on *his* piece of marsh. He lands nearby and begins an aggressive dance, hopping up and down, sticking his neck straight out at a belligerent angle to his body, and spreading his wings like a villain's cape. The two face off in this threatening manner, a few meters from each other, before the interloper relents and flies off croaking his displeasure.

The crowding of the marsh in the fall leads to the kind of aggression animal behaviorists observe in the laboratory and sociologists document in the inner city. I wonder at the energetic balance for the aggressor, who expends energy now for potential gain later, in protection of its larder. But this kind of aggression is unavoidable in September, it seems, when the migrants mingle, all with the selfsame purpose: to get fat before heading south. Perhaps there is a certain jitteriness, a case of "nerves," as we too experience before setting out on a long journey.

The stalking and jousting go on all day—to little avail, it seems. Whenever the interloper returns, the heron on territory assumes a hunched position, neck lowered and drawn back between its wings, and skulks through the wheat-colored grasses. Finally, it rushes at the other heron, raising its wings as it does and putting the run to its competitor.

Before, I considered such territoriality more typical of the spring breeding season, but clearly guarding feeding ground is also necessary as temperatures drop and migration approaches. Even this small, seemingly insignificant patch of marsh is worth a squabble, it seems, reminding me of the importance of saving such parcels of wild land, or, in the case of the Old Marsh, of returning appropriated land to its first, rightful owners.

Rivalries also occur between different species. A greater yellowlegs settles into a vacated marsh pool, announcing his arrival on the scene with a loud, unpolitic kipping. The irascible heron immediately cruises by to chase off his diminutive competitor. The yellowlegs, however, is not easily intimidated and immediately jumps up, dive-bombing the heron—which dolefully flies away.

There is even an irascibility in relations among species not in competition for food or locked in a mortal predator-prey role. Almost daily now I see a marsh hawk, either the paler male or the ruddy female, canting over the dyke, doing its rounds, crossing and recrossing the marsh borders. Its appearance— the gestalt of hawk—causes a commotion. The tattling yellowlegs raise the alarm, and the teal rocket into the air, though the harrier is seeking meadow voles and other rodents secreted in the grass.

I last saw marsh hawks in May, but now they return to hunt the Old Marsh in late summer. Their absence coincides with breeding season, when, I suspect, they are nesting on the nearby Tantramar Marsh. The second-largest breeding population in North America is resident there.

At the turn of the century, the Tantramar, at 20,000 hectares (about 50,000 acres), was known as "the world's largest hay field." Ninety percent of this former salt marsh had been dyked, first by the Acadians and then by Yorkshire immigrants when they occupied the dyke lands after the expulsion of 1755. Sheltered from the sea and its tides, the Tantramar produced so-called English hay rather than salt-meadow hay. It fueled horses on farms and in local coal mines and lumber camps and also filled schooner holds for export to the eastern seaboard, especially Boston. With the invention of the internal combustion engine and mass production of automobiles that followed World War I, "horsepower" took on a new meaning. The dyke lands went into commercial decline, and now only a handful of the iconic weathered barns figure the flat landscape of this maritime prairie. In recent decades, conservationists have clawed back small portions of the dyke lands, returning them to their natural state. The Tintamarre Wildlife Area now preserves a mosaic of wetlands where for centuries hay rakes and horses ruled. Today when I cross over this border region, I see a few beef cattle fattening on pasture but, almost always, marsh hawks surveying the flat fields. They find enough prey there to feed their young secreted in ground nests, but when the nestlings have fledged the hawks make their appearance farther afield, including on the Old Marsh.

September

The Old Marsh itself produced hay until thirty years ago, and my view then would have included a barn. Sherman waited until September to harvest the heavy salt-meadow hay.

Unlike my mother and father, who made their hay by hand, he turned it with his tractor and hay rake, trying to avoid miring the machines in drainage canals. "You didn't want to get the mowing machine in those ditches. Then you'd be in a hell of a mess." Or sinkholes. "You'd go down into one of those holes, with hay over it, and you'd curse and swear." The marsh hay was also slippery, sliding off the fork like silk as you tried to pitch it onto the wagon and into the mow.

Sherman harvested not only the marsh but the dyke, where he couldn't operate with machinery but had to use a scythe.

"That was the greatest place for bumblebees' nests you ever seen. You'd hear a lot of cursing and swearing and you'd know Jack or Jim ran into a bumblebee nest"—he laughs—"and they'd have a tale to tell when they came over for dinner."

After the hay was taken off and stored in the mow, Sherman removed the clapper on the *aboiteau* to allow the tide to flood the marsh, renewing its fertility. The barn had no floor, and often the spring tides would flood the barn. The hay, however, was protected, stacked on mows made of crisscrossed poles, allowing air to circulate underneath and keeping the hay relatively high and dry.

Eventually, Sherman took a day job in town, like my father and so many other small-time farmers who could no longer make a living on the land. The barn sills rotted, and twenty-five years ago he took the barn down, salvaging what materials he could. Today there is no trace of it. The *aboiteau* was intact (except for the clapper) when we moved here, but it too has become victim to the tides, collapsing into the marsh muds of the drainage canal.

The return of the sea has again made the Old Marsh a wild place, home to fishes, mammals, and birds, and vitally, in the spring and fall, a feeding ground for migrants.

For the migrants exploiting the marsh, September is a time of turmoil, of impending change. Weather-wise, it is hurricane season, for in the south, tropical storms (cyclones) are brewing in the warm waters of the mid-Atlantic. Most spend their fury when they "make land" on the Caribbean islands and southern coastal United States. But each year a few gather momentum as they spin northward along the eastern seaboard, smashing into Nova Scotia, which barely hangs onto the continent by the Tantramar Marsh and, where I grew up on the coast, exposes itself to the full battering of the open seas.

In 1954 Hurricane Hazel spun out of control and plunged into the heart of the continent, its 200-kilometer-per-hour (125-mile-per-hour) winds killing a hundred people in the United States and, accompanied by heavy rains, drowning thirty-five people on a single street in Toronto. Cathy remembers her street in the Toronto suburb of Don Valley running with water.

I stood alone at the low windows of the dining room, looking toward the apple orchard and the line of old spruce that marked one boundary of Brook Farm. The bubbles in the old panes, the sheeting rain, and the menacing winds pulsing against the glass distorted my view, but I was mesmerized by the metronomic oscillations of the tall trees. They bent in great arcs, first one way, then the other, crossing and recoiling, bowing down to the earth and catapulting back to the vertical.

Where was everybody? Perhaps my father had gone to the barn to batten the doors. The wind would take away his short breath! I was four years old. My brothers, my mother, were somewhere inside, in other rooms, surely. Perhaps my mother suddenly appeared from the adjoining kitchen to whisk me away from the window, which seemed poised to explode under the hurricane's pressure. But I have only this one memory—of the trees gone mad. Some would fall, their ocher-colored cores exposed. One toppled over a small brook that drained the cranberry bog, and my playmates and I used it as a bridge and in imagination converted it to a sailing ship for pirate games. The great gray corpses of the fallen trees formed a tangle where once there was a clear path, and I climbed over and under them, pretending I was a deer escaping a hunter's sight.

Hazel was what climatologists now call a hybrid storm, which occurs when a tropical storm, born at sea, combines with a continental low pressure system and, instead of blowing itself out, gains energy and ferocity as it moves northward. The most notorious example was the Saxby Gale, which swept into the Bay of Fundy on 150- to 175-kilometer-an-hour (90- to 110-mile-an-hour) winds on October 5, 1869.

It is notorious for two reasons: First, because it was so destructive. But second, Stephen Martin Saxby, in letters to *The Standard* of London, England, had predicted "equinoctial gales" throughout the world on that date, accompanied by very high spring tides. Although Saxby's theory that weather was controlled by phases of the moon was false, fortuitously his prediction held true in the Bay of Fundy when hurricane force winds combined with the highest tides of the month to wreak havoc along the Fundy coast.

The winds felled forests, blocking roads and railways, and blew vessels ashore, including the barque *Genii,* with the loss of eleven lives. In one New Brunswick village, a storm surge drove a schooner over the dykes into an orchard and its owners had to dig a canal to float it back to sea. Likely all of the Acadian dykes in the Minas Basin and Chignecto Bay (the two arms of the inner Bay of Fundy) were overtopped, and the Tantramar Marsh and the surrounding towns, including Amherst, and villages were flooded. In all, as many as a hundred lives were lost.

We speak of such events as "once in a century." Hurricanes, however, are becoming more frequent; the highest number of storms since records were kept occurred in the 1990s. In 1999 five tropical storms came ashore. By the time Hurricane Floyd strafed the Atlantic provinces, it had lost much of its power. The tops of the spartina, heavy with seed, bent in the winds under a pewter sky adumbrated with nimbus. A blue heron hunched in the marsh in his nimbus-colored cloak, while the teal wheeled around, seemingly unfazed by the gales. But days later Floyd's younger brother Harvey collided with Gert, unleashing a one-in-a-hundred-year rainfall.

I am on the Margaree River, on Cape Breton Island, when this "perfect storm" coalesces, seemingly out of nowhere. My salmon-fishing buddies and I retreat from the river, deep in the Highlands, and as we follow the dirt road wending through the mountains, we see trees tortured in the manner I remember of Hazel. Some are down already, beside but not blocking the road. The plastic lawn furniture on the verandah of our rented cottage is shunted from one side to another—like articles in the fo'c'sle of a storm-tossed ship—as we take shelter from the winds and the rains.

I call Cathy, who tells me that Tidnish Bridge has become an island. The three roads leading home have all washed out, and she has only made it to the house through a backwoods road that was also flooded minutes after she passed. More than 200 millimeters (8 inches) of rain have come down in two hours, causing the dam at Mosley's Pond, upriver, to burst, unleashing a torrent of water. Like the Saxby Gale, the storm is accompanied by spring tides, and the combination of tide and runoff has pushed water onto the lawn.

Friends Morris and Susan Haugg arrive to check on Cathy's safety. Morris, a native son of Bavaria, remarks that the normally placid Tidnish looks like the Danube in an angry state. The fire department is called out to sandbag our neighbors' basement; even so, Charles and Doris get 5 centimeters (2 inches) of water in the house.

We are spared, despite our folly of living on a flood plain, and by the time I arrive home the next day the flood waters have receded from the lawn, though the marsh is still submerged.

As it often does, the season turns in the wake of such tropical storms. They seem to take the warm summer air with them. The cooler air and still-warm waters manufacture mist in the mornings, and two days after Floyd and Gert move off to ravage Newfoundland, two large wedges of Canada geese pass overhead.

AUTUMN ENERGIES BUILD throughout September: more birds, more winds, more billowing cobalt clouds. In the leaner light, the marsh ponds shine like silver-nitrate plates fixing the black-and-white images of blue-winged teal. Each day the count increases, one dozen, two dozen, up to one hundred of these little ducks tipping up, fattening on the pondweed's carbohydrates. As Aristotle first noted 2,300 years ago, creatures fatten in the fall, preparing for migration. At the same time, some birds have already fled the northern marshes. I no longer hear the clarion cries of the willet or the gossipy chatter of swallows.

One of the vital roles of the salt marsh and its associated tidal pools and creeks is as a nursery for small fishes. An estuary, where salt and fresh waters mix, is ten times as productive as the open ocean, and the salt marsh is ten times as productive as the estuary. Small fish come here to feed and grow, as well as to seek shelter from larger, predatory fishes. Fully two-thirds of the catch of commercially important fishes spend part of their life cycle in estuaries. We have seen the smelts and gaspereaux come and go. Striped bass lurk in the estuary in summer, I'm told, and if I seined the tidal creeks, I'm sure I would snag young pollack and hake. Among the most important species to wild and human fishers is winter flounder. These fish migrate offshore to cooler waters in summer but in the autumn return to the estuary as the waters there begin to cool.

The flounder hide themselves under a coating of sea bottom sediments, with only their eyes—beady periscopes—projecting above the substrate. (In adults both eyes are positioned on the right side of the head, the left eye having migrated there as the young fish matured in accordance with the developmental miracle that produces a flatfish.) They lie on their pale left side; the darker topside—their right—has a remarkable capacity to change color to match the bottom where they take cover, presenting a formidable challenge to those wild fishers seeking them.

When I was a boy, in the summers when the trout were not biting, on a Sunday the family would travel to Yarmouth Bar to fish for flounder instead. We timed our departure to coincide with the low tide and stopped along the way to dig soft-shelled clams for bait in Yarmouth Harbour.

Holes made by their siphons indicated where the clams were hidden, and when Dad dug into the flats with his clam fork, often a telltale geyser of water would spout up, indicating a live clam secreted there. My brothers and I eagerly picked out the clams, with their smooth, bluish-white shells, and tossed them into a bucket. Gathering the clams (which in the harbor were too polluted to eat) was half the thrill of flounder fishing. We bent eagerly to the task, digging our fingers into the blue muds where a white shell shone through and sometimes aiming and squeezing the clam, converting it into a natural squirt gun, to soak each other. At the end of the clamming, we were usually coated with mud and clam juice, redolent of the seashore.

Then we made our way past weathered sea shanties, where fishermen stored their gear. These were ramshackle structures, abraded by the constant sea winds and salt, and beside them were stacked mountains of handmade, lath lobster pots, ready for the season, which would not open until the end of November. I remember my shock—a mixture of sadness and disbelief—when my mother said that one of these decrepit houses had once been her home, after her father had drowned in a winter storm, on February 28, 1922. Her widowed mother, it seems, had found refuge here with fisherfolk relatives. My mother was only two at the time, and her only memory is of her bedroom in a loft, which she reached through a trapdoor—a frightening image to her still. She could never remember which shanty it was, if in fact it was still standing. No one lived in them now, but I never passed those shanties (which to the tourist might seem picturesque) without thinking of her early tragedy—searching each weathered façade for some clue that this might be the one.

She was adopted by a prosperous butcher and his wife in town, and her mother remarried, settling in the Boston States, as Maritimers call New England. She spent her last years in a sanitarium, haunted by the image of her first husband, whose body was never found, miraculously returning across the years and seas—a living nightmare experienced by many fishing widows.

The shanties stood in the lee of a great breakwater, piled high with granite boulders the size of cars. Even so, waves sometimes breached it, when storms blew off the Atlantic, and as proof I found among the giant stones many ornate dog whelk shells, which had been torn from the sea bottom, thrown into the air, and deposited there. The brightly colored Cape Island fishing boats, in those days always named for wives and children, found safe haven at the Yarmouth Bar, where they were protected not only by the manmade breakwater at their back but by Cape Forchu, or Forked Cape, named by Samuel de Champlain when he sailed by here in 1603 on his voyage of discovery to New France.

The wharves jutted into the water on great pylons, which also supported storage sheds and chandleries painted a rusty red. We fished from the staging, which at low tide was 7.6 meters (25 feet) above the water to accommodate the great rise and fall of the Bay of Fundy tides. When I was very young, at my mother's urging, my father tied me to a pylon, looping rope through my belt. I felt like the little fisher boy whom I had seen in a schoolbook illustration—also tied to the wharf for his safety—but it was small compensation for being tethered while my older brothers moved about freely on the wharf.

We dropped our clam-baited hooks into the depths of the green-gray waters and waited for a tug. At low tide, we mostly caught sculpins that milled about the wharves, scavenging fish offal. Surely one of the ocean's ugliest creatures, they had broad spiny heads, the same length as their bodies, supplied with rows of teeth, fine and sharp as glass shards. Their fanlike pectoral fins waved in the air as we reeled them in, and their great mouths gaped wide as they gulped air, puffing up their flaccid bellies. Removing them from the hook was an exercise in caution, not only because of their teeth, but because of the spines that adorned their heads, backs, and bellies, any of which could inflict a painful wound. Their saving grace was their exotic coloring—speckled with red, yellow, and orange blotches, each fish displaying an idiosyncratic color scheme. We banged them on the wharf planking, and they flopped off our hooks, disappearing into the dark waters.

September

If we lost patience waiting for the flounder to bite, my brothers and I might raise our hooks off the bottom to try to catch the juvenile pollack that frequented the wharfs. These swift, torpedo-shaped fish, the pale green color of antique gin bottles, fought hard and often as not fell back into the water before we could reel them up. Or if we did bring them in, we released them anyway, as they were too small to clean and cook.

The large flounder moved inshore with the tides, and as the water rose up the pylons, we began to catch more and more of these powerful flatfish whose shape helped them hold to the bottom and made them hard to lift. The small ones we released, but some were the size of dinner plates, and occasionally we caught one that would fill a dinner platter. At the end of the day, my father would strip two fillets—a light one from the bottom, a dark-veined one from the top—with his hunting knife. When we returned home, we ate them fresh, savoring their tender, sweet flesh, which my mother fried in the butter that she had churned that morning.

MOST OF THE WINTER flounder that migrate into the Tidnish River estuary and up the river itself, beginning in September, are juveniles, about the size of my hand. This immigration attracts the attention of a variety of predators, avian and mammalian—and provides them with an important store of fat, either for migration or for the coming winter. Through the fall months, we are treated to a steady parade of fishers: mergansers, seals, great blue herons, and cormorants.

One morning Meg says with delight: "Look at the ducks!"

Three red-breasted mergansers cruise upriver in a regal line, scattering schools of panicking minnows in their wake, but it is the flounders they are seeking. A couple of days later, a bull harbor seal pokes his mottled head above the water. Well camouflaged by the silvery light, he looks around, then submerges, sinking straight down. He remains submerged for an impressive length of time, emerging a few hundred meters downriver.

From my study, I watch as a heron planes into the marsh for a landing, steady as a glider until it performs a startling maneuver. I am aghast as it suddenly tips 90 degrees, its pterodactyl wings banking vertically, then rotating back 180 degrees the other way—the great bird seems out of control, its gangly frame appearing to dissemble from wind sheer before my eyes. This urgent but awkward move stalls its momentum, and it dives toward the river, splashing down, then rising with a small flounder clamped in its scissoring beak.

Perhaps the most proficient of the winged fishers are the cormorants, for which they have been much despised and persecuted by humans who view them as competition, though numerous studies have shown their diet largely consists of "trash fish"—for example, sculpin, cunner, and eel in salt water; perch, bullheads, and carp in fresh water—of neither commercial nor recreational importance. In the fall, however, they do devour the flounder.

The Bard went so far as to accuse cormorants of being such gluttons they could "devour Time." There is nothing subtle about the double-crested cormorant, in either appearance or behavior. Milton likened the cormorant to "the Devil on life's highest tree." These large, dark birds do present a chilling picture when perched atop dying trees on their offshore breeding islands. Their devilish silhouette is dramatized by their practice of spreading their wings to allow them to dry; otherwise, they become waterlogged and reduce the bird's buoyancy. They are a primitive bird on the evolutionary scale, and as one bird biologist has noted, they have "an archaic look, not unlike that of

Archaeopteryx, the prototypic bird-reptile." Although not Jurassic in age, as a species they probably achieved their present body shape as long ago as 50 million years. As they hunch on a tree, their S-shaped neck presents the illusion of a snake that has been drawn through a bird's body. It ends in a hooked bill and, underneath, an orange, leathery pouch that can expand to accommodate largish fish.

A small flock of cormorants is feeding upriver, gorging on flounder. I am shocked at just how large a flounder, the size of two hands, these fish can force down their expandable throats. When one gets a fish too large to swallow with ease, others gather around and try to snatch it from its beak. All pretence of table manners is abandoned by this unruly crowd.

Their appearance and manners aside, they are consummate fishers. I watch as one of these dark-mantled seabirds demonstrates its effective, if eccentric, technique. It rears up, almost standing on the water, all the while paddling furiously to maintain its vertical position. The cormorant curls its neck back between its clavicles and tucks in its bill, apparently so that it can look straight down into the water, then dives and surfaces with a flounder flapping in its beak. It maneuvers the flatfish into position with its hook-tipped bill and swallows a great bulge, grotesque as a goiter appearing at the throat, and dives again. Sometimes I observe that a cormorant will ingest so many flounder at a feeding that it is too bottom-heavy to take off without a great spluttering effort, beating the river with its wings as it tries to gain altitude.

RING-BILLED GULLS show up on the marsh at the beginning of September and hang around for most of the month. My friend the nature writer Wayne Grady has cleverly dubbed the ring-billed as a "land gull," for its habit of following behind the plow, plucking worms and other invertebrates from the tilled soil. Smaller than the herring gull—the prototypical "seagull"—this member of the gull tribe bred primarily in the prairies before the 1920s, with just a few scattered colonies in the East. These gulls show the same predilection for garbage as their larger relative, however, and have reached the status of pest around the heavily settled Great Lakes and St. Lawrence River valley. They first bred in the Maritimes in the mid-1960s and have established colonies along the coast of the Gulf of St. Lawrence. The ones that predictably show up on the Old Marsh probably drift in from the three colonies on Prince Edward Island, a mere day trip across the Northumberland Strait. Although connoisseurs of fish offal and fast food litter, these dainty gulls come, it appears, to crop Charles's blueberry field, where I often see them circling in graceful gyres. They are not, however, above parasitizing a live meal from an unsuspecting merganser surfacing with a flounder in its saw-toothed beak.

Although the opportunistic habits of the gull clan are hardly praiseworthy, it is well to remember that their fortunes are intimately tied to our own lifestyle. Their population growth is directly related to our own wastefulness, dependent as they are on garbage, especially in the winter months.

Many of these marsh loafers, I observe, are also molting, dropping old feathers for new in preparation for their own movement south to warmer coastal areas. I welcome their return each fall for an unlikely reason: their guttural, unlovely voices. The sound of a protesting gull instantly establishes my connection to the sea. Their call is like the snap of an electrical impulse, activating an ancestral synapse in my brain. When I hear a gull's cry, I know that I am not far from salt water, from the sea, and that knowledge comforts me, affirms my chosen place in the world.

September

On a Sunday morning I am awakened at eight by an unidentified sound. Meg must be stirring is my first thought, but once my rational faculties kick in, I conclude that it is too early on the weekend for her to be up and around. I rise reluctantly and go outside to check the roof, where I have determined the sound seems to be originating. Nothing on the riverside, but when I go around to the front of the house and look up, there is a great black-backed gull with a flounder half stuffed, headfirst, into its beak. He has been doing a tap dance on the roof in his exertion to swallow the flatfish whole. The flounder transforms the gull's beak into a full-lipped visage. The great gull (the largest of its kind) regards me with this pallid grin, a sheepish smirk, as if it were embarrassed to have been caught in the act.

I know that nothing could be further from the truth, however. The great black-backed gull, whose common name is the parson, for its striking black-and-white coloring, is an unrepentant predator. On eider breeding islands in the St. Lawrence River, I have watched as these gulls nabbed eider chicks by the neck and tossed them into the air, nonchalantly catching and swallowing them whole—one after the other, as if they were eating peanuts. Certainly this fellow is unrepentant about disturbing my peace on the Sabbath. Disgruntled by my appearance on the scene, he flies off wearing his supercilious smile.

OTHER FISHES MOVE into the river in the late days of September. Our third fall on the marsh, while walking the dog by the river, I hear a series of splashes. Small fish seem to be feeding all over the river, occasionally flipping free of the water. I go down to the dock in the hopes of getting a better look. The moon lights up the river surface but not well enough for me to discern what size, let alone what type, of fishes are creating the commotion. I go back to the house for a flashlight. It, too, proves unsatisfactory, so I repair to the barn for the trouble light, which I rig up with a long extension cord, and train this brighter beacon on the subject. I fancy that I must present the picture of an Asian fisherman fishing by torchlight, employing cormorants tethered to my boat by strings to catch my fish for me, or something equally exotic, to my neighbors, who might wonder what the naturalist next door is up to now. I can see a few fingerlings; the light is strong enough not only to illuminate them but to penetrate them, so I can make out the blue lines of their backbones. But in the end, I am unable to solve the mystery. Could these fingerlings be responsible for the frenzied river sounds? I resolve to ask Sherman about this fall run of little fishes.

The following September, I am in the kitchen when I hear a bubbling of activity through the screened patio door. I know at once it is the little fish Sherman calls "shiners." I head down to the dock with flashlight in hand. The tide is flooding strongly, and, true to their name, the shiners flash silver in the light beam. The river surface is like a tin roof reverberating under a downpour. Fish are everywhere I look, and I can hear them up and down the river in the dark. A wondrous quantity of fish! In the distance I hear a heavy splash of a predator—mink, seal, striped bass, heron?

It seems these mystery fish only migrate at night, as I never see the phenomenon of their schooling during the daylight hours.

It is late at night when the river is again alive with the small shiners whose true identity has perplexed me for a decade. They have arrived earlier than usual this year, on Labor Day. As I always do, I repair to the house for a flashlight and to the garage for a fine-meshed smelt net. Although I have tried to dip them before without success, this time I manage to snag a couple of specimens. I return to the house to identify them, placing them in a saucer in my office to key out their identifying features. I feel somewhat self-conscious and clandestine about this task, which reminds me of my days in biology labs. I hear Meg up and around; she is unable to sleep with the prospect of the first day of school looming in the morning. I invite her into the study to share in my discovery. At first she is horrified, or feigns being so, as if she had discovered Dr. Frankenstein experimenting in her father's study. But she soon joins me in poring through the fish books. Comparing illustrations, we determine that these fat little fishes are striped killifish (or mummichog), *Fundulus majalis*, close relatives of the salt marsh resident *Fundulus heteroclitus*.

After our late-night seminar, Meg follows me back to the dock. She is wrapped in a fleece blanket against the autumn chill, but I want to share with her this phenomenon of the little fishes. They are still churning the water.

"Amazing," she allows. Then, turning her gaze to the night sky, she says, "Look at the Milky Way"—which shines resplendently through the clear September atmosphere.

"Look at how the stars are reflected on the river," I reply.

We fall silent watching the starlight phosphorescing on the river surface and the shiners leaping like little living stars.

FALL IS UPON US NOW. Great polarized cumulus clouds are shot through with the piercing September light and roll across the sky on blustery winds. Rimmed with the yellow heads of seaside goldenrod, the marsh border blazes like a field of ripe canola. That old man of the marsh, the bittern, is back, skulking through the spartina and hunkering down at the edge of the marsh pools. He seems as mesmerized as a horse asleep on its feet in the fields. He draws himself up into a sullen ball and stares into emptiness, only occasionally offering a disdainful glance at the ever-active yellowlegs strutting through the pools in pursuit of minnows. His back to the wind, the bittern seems disillusioned with the world

There are also calm, clear days in September, what we like to call Indian summer days, that may linger far into November. Each one is a gift. Sitting out by the river at dusk, I listen to the fall chorus: the low mumbling of ducks out of sight behind the dyke, the peeping of spotty sandpipers as they raft up-river—like proud saltwater captains—on eelgrass mats, the harsh exclamations of yellowlegs, the ratchety songs of land birds. The air is echoic, the sound traveling cleanly and resonating in the distance, downriver. Apples fall behind me with a muffled thud, and the moon, in its first quarter, rises bone white into the socket of the night. In the west, at my back, the apricot and salmon-pink mares' tails flare up from the cobalt-blue bank of cloud on the horizon.

The spartina is now russet topped. In the waning light, it seems to glow with its own incandescence, illuminating the night marsh like thousands of low-burning votive candles.

In the morning, after the first of fall's frosts, the river and marsh are shrouded in mist. But the last of the summer heat soon tears away this caul of nighttime, and out of this mysterious ether emerges a great blue heron—like the mist given form, congealed and animated.

10

October

THE SACRED HUNT

MUCH HAPPENS at the periphery of our vision, perceived but not noted. I know that I miss far more than I record. But the daily visual mantra of my marsh view captures rare moments.

I'm uncertain what first alerts me—ducks quacking alarm or the blur of the raptor itself plunging to the water, glimpsed through the riverside willows. I rush to the deck, binoculars in hand, to see the raptor circle over the marsh, then bank and drop like lead to where the ducks are drifting on the river. They dive in defense, avoiding the bird's terrible rushes on several occasions. (To fly, I think later, would only make them more vulnerable.) As I observe this drama unfolding, the question keeps surfacing, "Who is this swift hunter?" Finally, it veers away, though I do not see in which direction it goes or whether it has been successful in its raid.

When I check my bird books I realize the hunter could only be an immature peregrine falcon—the well-named duck hawk. (This bird was brown on the back, distinguishing it from the slate-back adult.) But it was the deadly speed of this hunter that marked it as a falcon.

Peregrines have been clocked at 320 kilometers per hour (200 miles per hour) when stooping, but probably half that speed is closer to the average. Regardless, it is very fast— the fastest speed achieved by any bird—and this speed accounts for its formidable hunting skills, exploited by falconers for centuries.

EVERY EVENT IN NATURE is merely a snapshot, a frozen moment, recording the flow of energy through the ecosystem. In trying to understand the dynamics of the Old Marsh, I learned very early to ask the obvious question, "What are they eating?" whenever I saw an animal, bird, or fish out my window. Over the years, when I discerned a pattern—such as the converging of flounder and fishers, both winged and furred, in the river and on the marsh in the fall—I began to understand that these meetings of predator and prey are an integral part of an annual cycle. Creatures must hunt for daily maintenance, of course, but their needs become more pressing at certain times of the year—in the spring, when they need more energy for breeding and raising young or for migration, and again in the fall, when birds, mammals, and fishes hunt to lay on fat for migration or, if they are staying put, for overwintering. For prey, the predator is also a necessary evil, culling the sick from the population and keeping numbers at a level that prevents the easy spread of disease or the overexploitation of resources. We call this equilibrium the balance of nature, though it is somewhat of a misnomer, as nature is above all dynamic, never entirely predictable or static.

This flow of energy is relentless, reducing everything by predation and decay to simple substances, which are taken up and recycled through the system. We, too, are subject to this transforming power; we, too, are on this conveyor belt of life force, moving from a state of being to extinction, as individuals and, ultimately, as a species.

FOR WILD CREATURES, their existential dilemma might be expressed in Hamlet-like terms: to eat or be eaten. In the fall, the feeding frenzy, like a medieval banquet, produces episodes dramatic and comedic, and on occasion both at the same time.

Before sunup a seal breaks the gilded mirror of the river surface and dives again. I walk upriver to the bend across from Sherman's and wait for the seal to reappear. Five minutes later its head pops up. The seal arches back its neck, thrusts its nostrils skyward, and inhales violently before submerging for another extended dive.

I am able to follow its progress upriver, as it produces a considerable wake in the shallow waters—like a moving school of large fish. This wake is of interest not only to me. The osprey is keeping watch from its favorite perch, atop the tallest spruce tree, 100 meters (325 feet) upriver from the bend. I watch with trepidation as it soars toward the river, descending with talons thrust forward. I know that the erstwhile predator might easily become prey if the seal turns its formidable jaws on the unsuspecting fish hawk, as seals sometimes do on seabirds, snagging them by the legs and pulling them under. The osprey descends but just as it is about to strike the water, its attitude and altitude suddenly change—this is no fish or school of fish. Realizing its mistake just in time, the startled bird quickly wheels away and retreats to its roost, its heart no doubt aflutter in its mottled breast, as mine had been moments before watching this misadventure unfold.

The next afternoon, the seal appears again on the advancing tide, this time floating on its back. Like a tourist on a gondola, he lets the tide push him along. His wet whiskers shine in the sun, and he wears an expression that is best described as serene contentment as he drifts by, unmolested this time.

THIS INTENSE SEASON serves up other comedic escapades.

The yellowlegs are feeding with the kind of vigor they bring to every task. You have to like this bird for all its over-the-top ways, whether tattling on and putting the bum's rush to overflying predators or pursuing minnows in the marsh pools. It does nothing by halves.

A yellowlegs chases minnows at the *aboiteau,* up to its breast in water. It charges through the water with its beak submerged, running in circles. The water ripples as the minnows make their escape.

I have observed this behavior before, and it strikes me that though the minnows may be the primary object of the yellowlegs' hot pursuit (and they are often successful fishers), it has the secondary benefit of stirring up invertebrates from the muddy marsh bottom—which the yellowlegs snags. In other words, there is method in this seeming madness. This food-procuring method, shared by avocets, is called scything.

Six other yellowlegs, immaculate and dandified, strike a pose on the marsh hillocks, which become tiny islands, loafing refuges, at high tide.

These birds lose all dignity when they go fishing, however. There is something almost mechanical about their quick stops and starts, their unexpected pirouettes. The comic nature of this dance is doubled when two perform a pas de deux and is re-doubled when several make up a predatory ballet de corps zigzagging through the shallows on those lean, namesake legs, their brilliant white bellies reflected in the marsh pool like frilly tutus.

The heron, of a more stately demeanor, faces its own peculiar challenges when fishing for flounder. Patrolling the river-bank at low tide, the heron strikes and impales a large flounder. What follows is a spectacle of predation, viciously effective but ultimately in vain. He carries the skewered flatfish to an exposed sandbar, drops it on its back, and repeatedly drives its bill into the fish's viscera. I am amazed at the heron's knowledge of the fish's vulnerable anatomy as it hammers at its heart and vital organs, releasing deltas of the victim's blood, which runs in rivulets over its exposed white underside.

The heron continues to hammer away but finds itself hoisted by its own petard, when it drives its daggerlike bill clean through the flounder and the flatfish will not come off. To extract itself from this predicament, the heron reaches up with one of its outsize feet—like a dog scratching itself behind the ear—and claws at the inopportune fish. After several increasingly desperate attempts, the heron rids itself of the burden.

The flounder is as big as two hands, and in the end the heron decides it is simply too much to swallow and walks off, leaving its kill for the crows or gulls to clean up.

During this fishing season I see crows fly by with small flounders in their beaks, which I assume they have scavenged. But I also see them dispatching live fish with a ferocity similar to the heron's. In the scope I observe a crow killing what appears to be a sculpin. It smashes away at the fish's armored skull with determined force, then flips it over and begins tearing out its gills; finally, opening the soft underbelly, it eviscerates the still-reflexing fish.

In the birds' defense, without hands there is no more tactful way of accomplishing these tasks. And our own methods of dispatching and disassembling animals is no less brutal, as I discovered on the front lines of a commercial slaughterhouse where I spent a day collecting blood samples for the vaccine development project I worked on as a veterinary research technician. The assembly line is an industrial nightmare, with workers quite literally bathed in blood, though the cows themselves are sent packing to their own Elysian Fields in an instant with a fatal bolt to the brain.

Killing animals on the farm and hunting were part of my rural upbringing, actions that did not elicit revulsion and censure in that culture or in me at that age. Even then I understood that slaughter was a necessary part—in fact, the object—of animal raising.

I did not witness the slaughter of any of our cows for meat and was not present when the herd was destroyed because of disease. Nor was I on hand for the annual slaughter of the pig that we raised on the skim milk that was the by-product of our cream production. But I helped my father slaughter a flock of chickens, and now I believe this must have been when we were finished with farming.

As a young boy, I had the job of collecting the eggs. It was a duty I enjoyed, not only because I took pride in helping out on the farm, but because of the peaceful aura of the chicken house. It was built on a cement foundation, unlike any of our other wooden farm buildings, and had been the piggery when my father produced more pigs for sale. The cement floor and knee-high wall made it easier to clean, I suppose. When I was a boy, we raised only the single pig for food in a pen built for it in a corner of the cow barn.

Dad had built nesting boxes for the chickens, attached to the wooden walls above the cement, which was still covered in a generous coating of whitewash. Bedding straw lay golden on the floor, where the chickens had kicked it from their nests. A strange hush always fell over the room when I walked in, the chickens looking up, their golden eyes glowing in the low light, and falling silent from their secretive conversations. I reached under their brown breasts to find the eggs warm to the touch. Likely they sometimes pecked at my hand in protest, but I do not remember this, merely their acquiescence, the almost eerie quiet.

When the time came, I also embraced the task of helping my father slaughter the chickens, out of a similar boyish pride in helping in this "man's work" of killing. We slaughtered the chickens in the woodshed, a dark building with a mud floor smelling of the earth and the rotting wood chips that were always strewn about. I caught the chickens and handed them to my father, who beheaded them on a chopping block, otherwise used for splitting kindling. I had known, as idiom described, that chickens ran around with their heads cut off, but it is hardly a spectacle for which one is prepared in the literal sense. Blood splattered onto the ground as my father's axe bit through the neck vertebrae— and the dead chicken exploded into a macabre dance before collapsing, as if it had only belatedly realized the finality of the act. The scene of the slaughter—stark images of blood, chaos, darkness—stand in sharp contrast to those I retain from the egg gathering—light, quiet, warmth.

Hunting was also complementary to the mixed farming economy that sustained us.

In October, at the start of hunting season, my father would carry his hunting rifle to the barn when he went to milk the cows in the predawn hours. The gun was an antique 1873 Winchester that might not have been out of place in a John Wayne movie. The barn overlooked the lower pasture and orchard, where sour windfall apples often attracted deer. As soon as the day brightened enough for Dad to sight the old rifle, a shot might ring out.

It was important for my father to kill this first deer to ensure a winter meat supply. On one occasion, my mother recalls, Dad shot the deer on the first day of the season before he bought a license, intending to get one on his way to work in town. He knew that if he did not shoot the deer then, some neighbor might before the day was done, and his own family would go without. He bled and quickly gutted the deer, saving the liver (a delicacy), which was sitting in a basin under the sink, still warm, when a salesman called. My mother was sure the unannounced visitor would sense the hidden organ, smell the blood I suppose, and know that her husband had broken the law, at least technically. The interloper never did, of course.

Dad saved a second deer tag for after the fall harvest and chores were done, when he and his friends in the community piled aboard a Model A truck with a jerry-rigged wagon tent over the truck bed and headed into the interior of Yarmouth County along the well-named Small Gains and Hard Scratch roads. They would return days later with buck deer tied over the hood of the truck and onto its rear bumper—if they were lucky, a deer to a man. In any case, the meat was apportioned equally and shared with friends and neighbors in the community who, for whatever reason, did not, or could no longer, hunt.

In the winter, I would clandestinely crawl out of my bed and lie on the cold linoleum floor, pressing my ear against the black, scrolled heat register to listen to the men reminisce about their fall hunting trips, the wood heat from the kitchen stove and their heroic, sometimes ribald, stories flying up together, warming my ear.

There was no ritualized expiation for the death of these animals, as in Native cultures, but everyone was grateful for the meat supply and understood a death was necessary to secure it. My father was adamant that a man never take a shot unless he was as certain as he could be that it would fell the deer instantly. If it all possible, that meant a head shot. A wounded deer could crawl away and suffer a slow death and, to make matters worse, might never be found, the meat wasted. There was a morality to these men, because, I think, they worked with animals daily and often loved them. Moreover, as practical men, they understood the need for conservation of meager resources, on the farm and in the wild.

Onetime hunters often make the most committed (and knowledgeable) conservationists. Theirs is an educated empathy because they have thought like animals in tracking them and have their individual deaths on their consciences, as I have the deaths of laboratory animals on mine. Even while still a hunter, a human being might be overcome by the moral dilemma that killing of any kind presents. My father admitted to once suffering "buck fever," a sudden unconscious aversion to kill that is a surprisingly common affliction among experienced hunters. With a buck deer in his sights, he once jacked all twelve shells out of the Winchester register, never once firing a shot, though he thought he had, in fact, heard the loud reports, felt the recoils, only to discover, sweating and disoriented, the unspent shells at his feet—and the deer still standing.

I never had the desire to hunt, or to be more honest, to fire a gun. Many of the games I played with my friends and brothers imitated hunting, however, with one of us assuming the role of the hunted—often a deer—and the others acting as the hunters.

It was a version of hide-and-seek, with a strong element of animism. But my aversion to guns arose from a too-real experience.

Gary had been in town all week at my grandparents', while I stayed home on the farm, where I was happiest. My father had loaded the Winchester and propped it in the porch as protection for my mother and me from an escaped convict who had been reported in the area. The decision to have a loaded gun in the house now seems so uncharacteristic of my father, who always broke it down after hunting and stored his ammunition separately. But the loaded gun stood there, this once, for my mother's and his peace of mind, while he was away during the day working in town. Back at home for the weekend, my brother saw it and did what was natural for a boy, picked it up and pointed it at me. It was a Sunday morning, and I faced him dressed in my church clothes.

Knowing what he could not know, I pleaded for him not to pull the trigger.

"It's loaded," I said. He did not seem convinced.

"Point it at the ceiling, it's loaded," I begged.

Seeing the fear in my face, he relented, and, pulling on the trigger, exploded a hole in the ceiling and the Sunday silence, the plaster raining down on our heads and blue blazers.

I heard my mother's cry, as she slumped on the stairs, and we ran to show her we were alive.

My brothers hunted for a time but never shot a deer—perhaps, they now believe, because they never wanted to. By the time we were grown men, hunting was a sport only, not as it had been for our father, a means of putting food on the table.

I remember the sweet smell of gun oil as my father cleaned the barrel with brush and chambray cloth. Even after my near-death experience, I imagined that I might someday follow in his footsteps, into the woods. I took a vicarious pride in his endeavor as he buttoned his red-and-black plaid mackinaw coat and cinched the homemade black leather bullet belt over his substantial girth and disappeared for the day into the backcountry.

If he was successful, he would hang the deer by the same block and tackle used to hoist the mow fork. The gutted deer hung head down, its gray tongue lolling lifelessly from its mouth, where blood still dripped intermittently, splattering sadly on cardboard that Dad had laid under the deer's head. The eyes were darkly opaque. Blood had crusted in the deer's ears— signaling a head shot. My pride in my father's prowess was now mixed with revulsion at the awful reality of the carcass, the transformation of this quick animal that I saw fleetingly in the back pasture into the dead.

But I ate the deer steaks and roasts as happily as everyone else, savoring their peculiarly rich flavor. And at the Christmas table, the deer, spiced with apples and cloves, appeared proudly in my mother's hands as a steaming mincemeat pie.

"HUNTING IS NOT JUST a central activity of the Cree, nor is it simply a science or a formal ritual. Hunting is an ongoing experience of truth as power," the anthropologist Harvey Feit has written. I experienced firsthand that power and truth among the Cree of James Bay when I joined the family of Gilbert Dick at his goose camp, on the shores of Manitounik Sound, where the migrating geese stopped to crop the grasses of the northern salt marshes.

One morning I heard geese calling and looked up to see a pair circling over the camp. The geese disappeared from view, then I heard the reports—three shots—from the hunters' guns. Near noon, Gilbert and one of his seven sons, Jacob, arrived back at the camp with two greater Canada geese, a large subspecies of the Canada goose.

Gilbert laid the limp birds on the boughs cushioning the tent floor. "They were a married couple, man and wife," he said, stretching out the longer neck of the male. Geese mate for life, he told me.

"You have to be a sharpshooter. If you don't kill them both, the other one would suffer too much."

Gilbert then drew my attention to the birds' wings. At the joints he had twisted together a primary from each wing, tying the two together. This is the first thing that a traditional hunter does when he downs a goose. "So the geese won't fly away," he explained.

He did not mean, of course, that these geese might come to life but that other geese might fly away and avoid his camp if he did not follow the traditional means of showing respect to the killed geese.

Gilbert, then forty-five, is a traditionalist who follows many of the hunting practices of his ancestors. Paramount among these is that the hunter show a proper respect for the animals. The foremost reason for this is that Cree believe that humans and animals are related (which they are, in the evolutionary sense), and that therefore one should show respect to them as one would to a person.

One means of showing respect is to ensure that there is no wastage of killed animals. I became aware of Gilbert's strict adherence to this rule the following day when I found him tending a boiling pot of bones. Among the disarticulated jumble of bones sticking out of the large aluminum pot was a caribou skull, displaying a fleshless grin.

"Only part of the animal we don't eat is the bones," Gilbert explained, catching my eye lingering over the pot. Even the bone marrow is mixed with dried fish chips to make a kind of pemmican.

October

"That's what the Indian people used to do in the old days. They would burn every bone. They didn't let them hang around the campsite so the animals could eat them.

"If you leave a lot of bones and the animals start eating them, that means that the bones of the animals won't come back to you. When you're a hunter, you have to be careful what you do with the animal. Every part of the animal has to be cleaned.

"Like with the caribou head I'm boiling," he said, returning his gaze to the boiling pot. "The meat will come off the bone and we will eat it, and then we will bury the bones.

"If you respect the animal, any animal, whenever you look for that animal again, you will find him very easily, but if you waste an animal, that means you will have a hard time finding him."

Gilbert put a stick on the fire to keep the pot of grinning bones at a rolling boil, then, taking his knife, cut and offered me a slice of hot caribou tongue.

ON A BEAUTIFUL fall Sunday, trees ablaze, Cathy, Meg, and I take the freighter canoe upriver, pushed by the incoming tide and a two-horsepower outboard. The river meanders, oxbowing around Lucius's Marsh, before straightening below a high river-bank and sandy plateau, the site of a devastating fire many years ago that is now covered by small jack pine. I look for and am pleased to still see the otter slide slithering down the steep bank. The river bends again at a 90-degree angle, narrowing be-tween white pines, black spruce, and poplar that grow to the river's edge. I look up to see an immature eagle, high atop a spruce tree.

"Look at the eagle," I say, pointing up.

"Watch out for that log," Cathy says, pointing down.

I cut power and we drift on the tide. Now there is something in the curved and buoyant shape that makes me think that it is

not a deadhead log but a body. It is hard to account for such ap-
prehensions, but I am right: it is a deer, a yearling or perhaps this
year's fawn, judging from the size. It drifts toward us like a cap-
sized barque. As we pull alongside, we can see that the deer is
missing an ear, probably the work of the scavenging eagle, which
reluctantly takes flight.

But how did the deer die? We had heard shots from upriver as
we set out, making me wonder whether someone had jumped
the opening of hunting season, in three weeks' time. But the animal had been in the water too long for that explanation to be
correct. It was waterlogged, not fresh. More likely, what we
heard was merely someone sighting their rifle in preparation for
the hunting season. Someone or something had killed this young
deer, however, perhaps as it was trying to make its escape across
the river, where it now drifted.

When we return down the river, the eagle has again taken up
its perch to protect its food supply.

Such disturbing images enter our unconscious, and that night
I dream that the deer has floated downriver and fetched up
under the dock. The rest of the dream's narrative slips away
when I wake, leaving only that premonition. I am skeptical, but I
nevertheless cannot resist checking whether the dream might be
a portent and immediately go down to the river. And there it is,
the deer body lodged against the dock's planking. I find a pole
and push the now-bloated carcass free, letting the tide take it on
its final journey to the sea and leaving me with the mystery of
intuition and the predictive power of dreaming.

Carl Jung believed that dreams "originate in a spirit that is
not quite human, but is rather a breath of nature—a spirit . . .
beautiful and generous . . . [and] cruel." Dreams, he said, cut
through the strata that have been built up by the rational, controlling tendencies of civilization to some deeper aspect of our

psyche, a more intuitive, instinctive place once the purview of so-called primitive societies. He believed, as I do, that maintaining such connections is necessary and healing. Dreams perform that function, as do firsthand encounters with nature.

For most of us, unfortunately, dreams long ago lost all of their practical power. Not so for the Cree hunters of northeast British Columbia, who, according to anthropologist Hugh Brody, once used dreaming to locate animals. He writes of this power in his book *Maps and Dreams:*

> *They located their prey in dreams, found their trails, and made dream kills. Then, the next day, or a few days later, whenever it seemed auspicious to do so, they could go out, find the trail, re-encounter the animal, and collect the kill.*

Good hunting, he was told, depended upon such dream knowledge.

SOMETIMES, NATURE seems to catch its breath, if briefly. For a short time, in the animal world, the dictum of eat or be eaten is suspended. At these times, I can regard nature without analyzing how it works or caring why. Thoreau wrote of this seeming state of grace: "This is a delicious evening, when the whole body is one sense, and imbibes delight through every pore. I go and come with a strange liberty in Nature, a part of herself."

I make this note in my journal after returning from the Tidnish Dock one evening in mid-October. I go there this time of year to enjoy the impressive congregations, on shore and in the water. At least a dozen gray spotted harbor seals are usually to be seen, and nearby a few of their larger, paler cousins, gray seals.

The fact that seals haul out here, rather than ships, is a historical irony, for this was to be the terminus of Henry Ketchum's ship railway. When I first visited the site, which is now a provincial picnic park, rusted steel rails still projected from the eroded point of land, suspended there as if to lead a phantom steam engine to ruin. Offshore, the artificial basin dug out to receive the ships that were intended to be pulled across the isthmus, from the Bay of Fundy to the Northumberland Strait, is clearly visible. The rim of this basin, exposed at low tide, is where the seals like to bask in the last warm rays of an Indian summer day. As they rest on the rocks, their upturned tails and heads give them the profile of beached sea kayaks.

I do not come only to see the seals. Spreading out their dramatic wings to dry in the sun, cormorants rest on the rocks, as do several herons, both for a time sated by fishing in the rich, shallow waters of the strait. The herons hunch their long necks between their shoulders and sleep. Offshore, dozens of red-breasted mergansers raft up, as well as scattered smaller flocks of red-throated and common loons, which are already beginning to adopt their grayish winter plumage. Their voices carry through the clear air as if through the thin walls of a bedroom. And usually several hundred Canada geese drift on the becalmed cerulean waters. Soon all will move south, but for now they rest.

Such an evening seems to offer a reprieve from the frenzy to forage and survive. I have a fellow feeling with all these creatures—seals, cormorants, herons, and seabirds. They are enjoying liberty, however briefly, from the food chain. For the human imbibing nature, becoming, as Thoreau enthused, "a part of herself," it is liberty of another kind—a fleeting freedom from oneself, a "strange liberty" indeed.

I HAVE ALWAYS LOVED the fall the best of all the seasons, even though it portends winter, a winding down toward ice and dormancy. But there are still delights and surprises before the marsh shuts down for the season like a seaside tourist motel.

In the morning there are hooded mergansers (last seen in March) cruising through the sepia-colored river mist. They pump their heads up and down in a haughty manner, the white crests of the males reflecting the early light like bright crowns. The pale stripes on their backs add to the royal demeanor of this magnificent species, making them appear robed in sable. Like a grateful subject, I welcome their return.

Then one morning a heavy frost encircles the grasses and the first skim of ice temporarily seals the marsh pools. In the sky there is the glower of November, gray nimbus clouds like a ledge of overhanging slate. My three crows take up their winter stations. A blue heron, the color of the impending month, flies poker-straight into a nor'easter.

The winds strip the maples of the last of their fiery leaves. Only the poplars cling to their harvest pumpkin colors. Columns of rain march across the Old Marsh, and the wind-driven tides mount the lawn. Ravens and a lone bald eagle—monochromatic as abstractions—brave the otherwise flightless skies. Near dark I look out to see a pair of hooded mergansers in the flooded marsh pool, their white crests sharply visible even through the gathering darkness and veils of cold rain.

In the fall the otters, which have spent the summer somewhere upriver, also return to brackish waters for the flounder feast. There are now pups with the adults, who are passing on their fishing acumen to this year's young. Through the scope I watch them dive, then manipulate the fish in their mouths with their fastidious hands, before chomping the flounder down, headfirst. Outside on the deck, I can hear the sound of their fearsome teeth, slicing through and crushing the flatfish's bones, echoing across the water.

11

OUT OF PLACE

THE PREVAILING winds turn around, from the southwest, backing into the northeast. They drive cold rain mixed with wet snow off the gulf and push the already-high spring tides farther up the shoreline and the river. The Old Marsh is drowned on such days.

Our first year here, the winds deliver more than bad weather.

A knock comes at our door around eight o'clock, and an eight-year-old, Aaron, his father, Dick, and his older sister, Bridget, are there with the news that a whale has stranded at Jackson Point, at the mouth of the river. The wind is blowing so hard that it nearly rips the storm door from my hands as I open it to let them in. Meg and I don rain gear and gather flashlights, and we all pile into Dick's car. We follow the Jackson Point road, lined with deserted cottages battened down for the winter, to the end and walk into the night. The rain and salt spume off the bay cut into our eyes, and our flashlights are impotent in penetrating the darkness. A swollen creek separates the road from the far beach, and in the pitch-black Dick and I don't dare try to ford it with the children.

No one seems to know for sure whether the whale is dead or still alive; the story circulating in the community informs us only that a whale has "beached." Where exactly, we don't know. We will have to wait until morning to discover the whale's fate.

The day dawns clear in the wake of the storm, so before school we drive again to the end of the road, where our search had stopped. There, meters from the other side of the creek, is the body of the beached whale, which, hours before, had been hidden from us by the slanting rain and the darkness, impenetrable and menacing as the cross-hatching in a Goya lithograph.

Dick and I can now easily wade the creek, hiking the children over on our backs, for a closer look at the stranded mammal.

It is a small minke whale, about 6 meters (20 feet) long. There is a series of short, straight marks behind its head and a trailing sinusoidal scar down its side; only in a couple of places, however, is the skin actually broken, exposing dark muscle underneath. My first thought is that it had been struck by a propeller (but who would be out in a small boat on such a night?); a large ship would have left a deeper gash. On its pale belly is a cross-hatching of smaller contusions, testament to the giant mammal's awful last struggle upon beaching, as is the edema, which gives to the belly a bloody and bruised appearance. Its left eye (the whale lies on its right side) is closed in death. The baleen visible in the whale's final, gape-mouthed repose is white and elastic, very much the consistency of plastic, which formerly recommended it for many uses, such as corset stays and clock springs.

An animal like a whale—likely as intelligent as us and of such imposing size—is profoundly disturbing in death. Yet there is a conflicting sense of event; this accident in nature has delivered a magnificent curiosity to our doorstep. It is hard to repress exhilaration at this happening. Such an uncomfortable emotion arises, I think, from our curiosity. The children, in their uninhibited way, circle the minke, poking it with their fingers, assaying its awesome bulk, scanning it as if to define what "whale" is, a foreign body that has crashed on the beach like a marine *Hindenburg*. Alternately, they stroke its rubbery skin—as if to comfort its spirit somehow.

This stranding revives for me the loss and helplessness I felt when fifty-eight pilot whales fatally stranded at Port Maitland Beach, near my childhood home, in 1960, when I was ten. I walked among the black corpses bloodied by their own vain thrashings and in some cases by callous observers who had actually carved their initials into the dead whales' bodies. I was dazed and amazed at the same time; I was in shock. But like so many coastal people before me, I asked myself: "Why did these magnificent marine mammals come ashore?" And why so many? It was an inquiry first posed by Aristotle in the third century BC that, even today, has not been answered satisfactorily.

It was several years after the minke stranded at Jackson Point that I went in search of answers to these questions and ironically found myself back in the pathology department of the Ontario Veterinary College, where twenty years before I had worked. I had known the whale-stranding expert, Dr. Joseph Geraci, in a casual way, enough to exchange courtesies in the coffee room. He had just published the most comprehensive study of why whales and other marine mammals, like seals and dolphins, come ashore, the culmination of three decades of field and laboratory research.

As with me, a morbid boyhood experience had sparked his fascination. Ever since a headless seal had washed up near his childhood home in Massachusetts, Geraci had been in search of the explanation for these mysterious events. There are two types: mass strandings, such as the pilot whales on Port Maitland Beach, and single strandings, as with the minke near my home. Nearly all mass strandings involve toothed whales (*Odontoceti*), including white-sided dolphins, pilot whales, and false killer whales. Baleen whales, such as the minke, almost always strand singly.

Toothed whales are highly social, deep water species, generally unfamiliar with shallower coastal waters. Regardless of species, singly stranded animals almost invariably are diseased or riddled with parasites, whereas, for the most part, mass stranded animals are normal and healthy.

In general, this is what was known. Geraci admitted to me straightaway that no one reason could account for all strandings—he had not found the Holy Grail of stranding theories. But he had debunked certain common theories by his exhaustive study of stranding events, which had him flying from coast to coast to wherever marine mammals came ashore.

One popular and logical notion is that toothed whales strand when chasing food, like squid or herring, in shallow waters. The problem with this so-called inshore feeding theory, said Geraci, is that dissecting the stomachs of thousands of fatally stranded animals has shown that the combined contents would not fill a shopping bag. Most animals that strand are apparently not feeding immediately before coming ashore.

According to a three-decade-old theory, storm conditions or ship noises might impair the toothed whales' echolocation mechanism, which helps them find prey and avoid objects in the water like nets. We now know, however, that their sonar is so precise that they can discern the contours of an object the size of a dime. As well, they have acute vision. It appears, noted Geraci, that they are not as lost as this theory suggests.

Parasites have been implicated. A type of lungworm that wends its way from the nasal sinuses into the middle ear, entwining itself around the middle ear, another theory goes, impairs their hearing. But almost all cetaceans—those that do and those that don't strand—harbor these worms that seemingly cause nothing more than a mild inflammation.

Magnetic anomalies along certain sections of coastline have been blamed. Some cetaceans do have magnetic crystals in the covering of their brains, like birds, but the evidence that their magnetic maps are disrupted by such anomalies is weak.

My favorite theory is the least refutable because it is so far-fetched. One theorist believed that primitive cetaceans, which evolved from the land to the sea, sought refuge on land when stressed and that this atavistic response might have persisted to this day, despite the fact that natural selection would likely have eliminated such self-destructive behavior long ago.

Geraci believed that there might be elements of truth in each of these theories—even the last, which at least accounts for the apparent determination with which marine mammals come ashore in the first place.

If not the why, what Geraci had been able to determine is what happens to marine mammals once they do come ashore. His findings are confounding and counterintuitive, but they do explain why attempts to rescue stranded marine mammals are so seldom successful. Even apparently healthy animals returned to the sea by rescuers or the tides often strand again, seemingly compelled to come ashore.

November

Stranded cetaceans, he learned, undergo a hormonal-induced, cascading stress response, resulting in failure of the circulatory system. This robs the vital organs of oxygen, including the liver, which is no longer able to rid the body of toxins. The whole metabolism of the animal spins dangerously out of control.

Ironically, this stress response is designed to isolate the animal from the marine environment, which, Geraci notes, is an inherently hostile place for a sick mammal—even a marine mammal—since it provides no refuge, whereas on land a mammal may hide until it feels better. In essence, once ashore, the whale battens the hatches and locks out its native sea. Often the fatal final act of the beached whale is to drink sea water. The whale normally derives most of its fresh water from its feed. The stress hormone aldosterone helps the animal retain water as it lies prone on the beach, but under prolonged stress, this short-term response works against the whale, since aldosterone also drives the thirst response. In time, the whale drinks—and dies.

IN ALL PROBABILITY this scenario describes what happened to the minke as we searched for it in the darkness and rain. There is nothing to be done now, however, and the children, whale aficionados all, want a souvenir—in particular, a piece of the cutaneous baleen that the living animal used to sieve its feed from the water. Pulling out a piece of baleen from the whale's jaw is like extracting a molar with one's bare hands. I have a pocket knife but repress my urge to satisfy the children's whim. I simply don't want to desecrate the body, though I feel guilty at not giving in to an innocent pleasure.

With similar sentiment I avoid taking a picture of the children with the whale. Would I take a picture of them with any other dead animal, except a fish? I take many shots of the dead whale, by itself, however, clicking away with a clinical obsessiveness, shooting it from many angles, as a crime photographer would record a murder victim as part of a forensic investigation. This information gathering, admittedly, serves another purpose: it somehow objectifies the experience, mollifying my own mixed emotions.

Later that day a whale researcher will arrive to perform an autopsy on the dead whale and declare it a healthy animal. Its reason for coming ashore will remain a mystery.

FOR WHATEVER REASON, the minke was disoriented—my best guess being because of the storm that lashed the coast that night, muddying the waters, creating a submarine din.

Other animals are driven out of their place by human action, as I discover when I arrive home one night to find a large buck standing in our driveway, the first time I have seen a deer on this side of the river. I should not be so surprised, for in November I have learned to drive the road through Tyndal Woods, from Amherst to Tidnish Bridge, with greater caution, as I am more likely to see deer in the ditches than at any other time of the year. In hunting season, the deer, I observe, move onto the road, out of the woods, where their gun-toting pursuers, looking like postapocalyptic survivalists in their camouflage gear, track them through the first fall of snow.

As the season turns toward winter, other creatures also seem displaced, or at least they are in new places. Each day when I walk the dog, I cross over a footbridge my neighbor Charles has built over the small creek that divides his property. Always, I stop and look down to see what fish might be there; in spring there are smelts preparing to make their spawning run upriver and, rarely, small brook trout, also returning to fresh water from the salt waters of the estuary. Usually there are a few minnows that dart for cover under the bank if my shadow falls over them. But in November, I discover a remarkable congregation of three-spined sticklebacks thronging the creek. The thick schools blacken the water, from the river mouth all the way to the road, a massing some 50 meters (165 feet) long by a meter (3½ feet) wide. I only observe them there in such impressive numbers during this month.

At first I think they must be spawning aggregations, but sticklebacks breed in summer. I conclude that the sticklebacks are merely seeking refuge in the shallow creek waters. Here they are safe from their hunters, the diving ducks—in particular, the hooded mergansers that patrol the river in November. The creek, shallow even when flooded by the tide, is less than ideal hunting territory, it seems, for these divers. As well, blue herons, devastatingly efficient in snagging such small fishes, are wary birds that avoid our side of the river where the creek empties into it. The constant pressure of these fishers must drive the sticklebacks from the main river into this hiding place. Such schooling behavior also is a survival tactic for individual fish; safety in numbers increases their chance of survival in case of attack.

The fishing pressure continues unabated well into the month. Hooded mergansers are joined by their larger cousins, common and red-breasted mergansers, which congregate at the river mouth but make feeding forays upriver. These winged fishers are joined by otters and harbor seals, drawn by flounder and smelts, which are reoccupying their wintering habitat in the estuary.

For some, however, the fishing season is drawing to a close. By mid-November (sometimes earlier) ice begins to form on the marsh pools. First it is merely a skim of ice that evaporates by midmorning. As the days grow incrementally colder and the hours of sunlight decrease, the ice lasts longer, eventually sealing the marsh pools. This closing down of their fishing grounds triggers the departure of the yellowlegs, which have lingered longer on the marsh than other shorebirds. When they finally embark on their belated migration, the marsh falls eerily silent.

The water itself is undergoing displacement. As winter approaches, the surface layers of water cool and, being heavier, sink, forcing up warmer layers from the bottom. They carry nutrients into the light zone, fueling a phytoplankton bloom in the late fall and providing a banquet for plankton-eating fishes like smelts and for filter-feeding invertebrates, such as mussels.

This late spike in productivity accounts for the congregations of waterfowl and sea ducks at the mouth of the river. Driving by on my return from the country store, I see a large raft of dark birds, like a thick line inked on the horizon.

I return to the house for the scope: at least a thousand Canada geese are gorging on eelgrass near the shore, and another two to three hundred red-breasted mergansers, with a few commons mixed in, are diving for smelts. Together they make a discordant chorus that is not only unmusical but "unbirdlike." The low, guttural utterances of the mergansers approximate a frog pond on a spring night. This droning is punctuated by the barking, at various pitches, of the Canadas. The geese are concentrated in dark masses (rafts), while the mergansers are more thinly spread out, stippling the bay. In the distance I can see that as many birds are amassed on the far shore.

Now I make a point of checking on these congregations on my daily visits to the store. Flocks of black ducks feeding on molluscs occasionally join the Canadas, and the mergansers come and go, some days numbering in the hundreds, the next, absent. The geese, at least, will stay until the end of the month or until ice glazes the bay—whichever comes first—forcing them southward in search of open waters along the Atlantic seaboard.

THERE ARE STILL DAYS when winter seems a remote idea, late Indian summer days when the contrast between the golden-and-russet-hued marsh and the blue water is stronger than at any other time of year. On such a remarkable late November day, I look out the window to see a seal head bob up. Judging from its size, it is a large harbor seal. It cruises by the house and then retreats slowly toward the sea. It seems in no hurry on this Sunday afternoon and, like its terrestrial mammalian relatives, seems intent on soaking up the last warmth of the season, making slow, leisurely dives while drifting on the tide. I watch from the River Room with the scope and see it surface with a large fish; yellowish and rotund, it seems like a sucker. To get a better look at the seal I skirt the river and hide in a copse of pasture spruce and poplar for a close-up view of its exploits. Sensing my presence, perhaps, the seal never shows again, sounding until he is out of sight around the river bend. Scanning the water for him, I spy an uncommon visitant. It is a white duck with a remarkably long tail feather (as long as a cock pheasant's), a light pink bill, and flowing body feathers. This dainty duck, delicate almost to a fault, dives intermittently and doesn't seem the least perturbed by my watchfulness. It sits high on the water with a perfect buoyancy.

It is a first sighting, and I must consult my bird guide to discover it is an oldsquaw duck. I read that it breeds in the Arctic and subarctic regions and winters in sheltered nearshore regions, such as Nova Scotia's South Shore, which is dotted with islands and indented with deep drowned coastal valleys. Despite their delicate appearance, they are prodigious divers, sometimes sounding to depths of 60 meters (200 feet) or more, for molluscs.

There is a certain irony to my ignorance. The call of the old-squaw is described as "cockawee" or "cockawit," which is the origin of the epithet Cockerwitters—the name given to my mother's people from Cape Sable Island and environs. They are distinguished by the way they talk, not only with their hands and at high speed, as my mother does, but by the idiosyncratic use of language itself, a language rich in metaphor and invention. Linguist Lewis J. Poetet, in *The South Shore Phrase Book: A Nova Scotia Dictionary,* describes it as having "descended from the language of Renaissance England, through dialects of northern England and New England."

The confusing etymology of "Cockerwitter" seems to take root in the diversity of ethnic influences that have shaped this wind-strafed, rocky, and often foggy, if linguistically enriched, region. The origin of the word encapsulates the colonial history of the sea-girt peninsula of Nova Scotia. On the great circle route of the North Atlantic, it became a collection place for displaced peoples—French, English, Scottish, Irish, and German—escaping the persecutions of imperial Europe, who in their turn displaced the aboriginal peoples, who, we know, have been here since the glacial ice retreated.

One historian says "cockerwit" may have its origin in the Algonquin-Mi'kmaq word *kakawegech,* meaning "wild duck"; another, in the French-sounding word *coquewit* or its Acadian variant. For me, the naturalist, the most plausible explanation is that it derives from the call of the oldsquaw duck—*cock-a-wee.* Its Latin name (*Clangula hyemalis*) means "noisy winter duck"—which might also describe the voluble speaking manner of the Cockerwitter. It is a label my mother and her fellow islanders now wear proudly, but it probably was originally an insult, comparing the "ungainly waddle of the duck" to the "awkward land-gait of the sailor," says *The South Shore Phrase Book.*

The appearance of the oldsquaw makes me contemplate the extraordinary hold this province has on its native sons and daughters. Ruefully referred to as Nova Scarcity by our forebears, in its four-hundred-year history Nova Scotia has enjoyed little economic prosperity, except for the brief decades in the mid-nineteenth century when its wooden ships were on all the world's oceans. In this century, Nova Scotians routinely fled to the Boston States, or more recently, central and western Canada, in search of a better, more secure life for themselves and their families. Yet just as many return or, like me, are never able to leave in the first place. The reasons for the almost congenital attachment to this place are not immediately obvious. Much of the soil is rocky and infertile; the original Acadian forests have been depleted, first by the British navy in search of mast trees, later by lumber barons, and now by the clear-cutting practices of pulp companies. In the last two decades, the once-legendary groundfish stocks have been hauled from the sea by factory trawlers to the point of commercial extinction. Yet we return and stay.

I feel a rootedness here, which is cemented by historical and family ties but which arises first in the landscape, I think. When we moved to our present home, with its view of the Old Marsh, I was returning to the landscape of my childhood. In *An American Childhood,* Annie Dillard writes, "When everything else has gone from my brain ... what will be left, I believe, is topology: the dreaming memory of land as it lay this way and that." The grip of the landscape, our own special place, is the last thing to let go.

My attachment to the salt marsh is more than nostalgic or cultural. It is visceral and instinctive. As for the herons, the foxes, and the fishes, this is my habitat, or that is how I feel about it when I look out at its green mantle of saltwater grasses, the dark eyes of the marsh pools, and the tidal river, the salt marsh's nourishing umbilicus to the mothering sea.

THE SIREN CALL of the sea grew louder after we moved from Brook Farm to the historic seaport of Yarmouth. Yarmouth Har- bour lay at the foot of the town and my street, and the gulls drifted up from the fishing wharves, serenading the townsfolk with their constant hungry cries. Many restless nights I lay awake, listening to the bellow of the diaphone foghorn, broadcasting its basso profundo warnings at the mouth of the harbor. Rather than barques, schooners, and clipper ships, the waterfront now berthed Cape Island lobster boats, as well as small groundfish trawlers, scallop draggers, and herring seiners. But in my imagination, Yarmouth was what it had been a century before, a world-class shipping center with its sea captains sailing their vessels to farflung ports, from Rangoon to Rio de Janeiro. Against all reason, I fantasized that I might still stow away on some tramp steamer for passage to such faraway, exotic places.

Town was anathema: linear streets and closely spaced houses hemmed me in, mentally as well as physically. One had to walk in straight lines, turn corners at predetermined places. I could no longer meander, like a slow river, seeing where the morning led me, along what crooked path to an enounter with a wild bird or animal.

At first, my reaction to this exile was illness, a homesickness not only of the heart but of the body. For two months I lay on a daybed, in the bay window of my new home, looking disconsolately at the strange and to me barren streets of Yarmouth town, while I battled strep throat and what I can only now describe as a profound depression. Although I recovered after a two-month convalescence, I never quite got over the longing to return to that place between the tides.

November

THE APPEARANCE of the oldsquaw in its winter plumage seems to presage the coming of winter, for the next day the first pack ice makes its way up the river.

November is a month of attrition, as the deteriorating weather displaces one species after another. The summer cottagers are the first to leave. The yellowlegs, as I've said, depart after the icing up of the marsh pools. A few green-winged and blue-winged teal mill apprehensively about the frozen fringes of the marsh before taking their leave for the open harbors of the Atlantic coast. Migratory flights of black ducks and Canada geese deplete the rafts of waterfowl in the estuary. The hooded mergansers quit the river rather than negotiate its treacherous ice flows.

The circle of the year is beginning to close. Some species, like the ducks and shorebirds, I will not see again until spring rolls around. This going away and coming back, the migratory pattern of this place, forms what I call the big picture. But underlying this seasonal rhythm is the diurnal cycle of the tides, their coming and going being the minor note, the constant melody that resonates with the larger movements. These rhythms, large and small, are comforting in their constancy, regardless of the vicissitudes of my daily life in the human-centered world or the challenges to my health, finances, or human relationships that might occur, year to year.

Now other familiar animals and birds move into view, reoccupying the niches abandoned by the summer residents and migrants, and compensating for their too-sudden disappearance. A red-tailed hawk soars over the tree line, beginning its daily rounds of its winter hunting territory. The foxes, which have only been fleetingly present since early summer, return from the deep woods to their marsh haunt. Already one of the White Birch progeny is sporting a magnificent winter coat, its tail nearly the same diameter as its body. As I watch the fox light-foot it over a marsh pool capped by ice no thicker than a window pane, I am reminded that the fox's size is an illusion—its bulk being mostly fur.

Even with the diversity of species diminishing as winter blasts its first harsh signals, the marsh serves up its share of drama. Several years after the minke whale strands, a white-sided dolphin also comes ashore in November, this time in the river itself. I only learn of this later, for some reason the news having not traveled upriver. No doubt it was fishing for smelts—the inshore feeding theory—but why it stranded I'll never know.

Certainly other marine mammals are still active in the river. Harbor seals continue to make inland excursions, even after ice begins to creep out from the riverbank. I see the great body of a seal, torpedoing under the ice, which is thin enough that if it needed to, the seal could butt a breathing hole in it with its head.

AT BREAKFAST, which we often eat in the River Room for its view, the sun flares overtop of the evergreens, crimsoning them. I look out to see what I think at first are two crows scavenging near the far marsh edge, below the fox den. But there is something about the shape—a curvature of back?—that is more animal than bird. I go to the scope but can't locate the form.

"There it is," Cathy says. "No, it's gone again."

I swing the scope across the field of vision and finally zero in, focusing on an otter.

It is diving into the marsh pool, disappearing and appearing, poking its oily head up through the shell ice, contentedly chomping on what can only be minnows, mummichogs perhaps that had not yet burrowed into the mud for the winter. It is a strategy I have never seen otters employ before, having always observed them feeding in the river, as their name, river otter, suggests. It is yet another example of the adaptability of animals, their clever opportunism in the face of adversity.

"It's enjoying appetizers," Cathy says.

NOVEMBER IS MY LEAST favorite month, rivaling the cruel character of April in Maritime Canada. The sky has the roiled, sooty look of industrial pollution. In most lights, the marsh is a pallid parody of itself, all color and vitality apparently sucked out of it. Yet wildlife continues to exploit the marsh, to forestall the inevitable.

Most years at least one great blue heron—its slate back mimicking the color of the month—perseveres until the bitter end. It commands my attention and excites my concern, as the days grow shorter and correspondingly colder. Like the other winged fishers, it seems as if it should be gone south by now.

The heron's favorite fishing spot is the *aboiteau*. Here the marsh drains constantly between high tides, carrying a never-ending supply of nutrients and discouraging the formation of ice. The sticklebacks pool here to feed and for the heron make easy pickings.

The heron's yellow eye shines in the westerly light as it plucks one after another of the prickly little fish from the shallow water. I count as it strikes five times in a row, never missing. On one occasion, it comes up with not one but two sticklebacks in that awesome beak, dropping one as it tries to swallow. The heron shakes its head each time after swallowing, seeming to savor its catch, the neck pulsating rhythmically as the spiny fish makes the long journey down.

The heron cleverly ensconces itself behind a little island of spartina, which has taken root in the fine muck that accumulates there. I wonder, too, whether its nimbostratus coloring helps camouflage this wader against the gunmetal gray skies.

With the marsh pools now frozen over, at least until midday, the great fisher camps out at the *aboiteau* every morning. My concern for its welfare grows as the first flotillas of ice begin ferrying up and down the river, congealing and breaking apart as they come and go. Ice or no ice, the heron stays, day after shortening day. It has no competition now, I reason; still, I wonder whether the cold does not more than offset its fishing gains.

AN ICE STORM BLOWS off the gulf near month's end, and the first snowfall that follows stays on the ground. These first wet, heavy flakes also cling to the evergreens, prompting Meg to say: "They look like they're covered in plaster of paris." In the wake of the storm, a massive tide pushes upriver, inundating the marsh. This proves to be good news for the crows, which have been keeping the heron company, sometimes themselves successfully stabbing a stickleback, which they tear apart before eating, holding the fish against a driftwood perch while they dissect it. The flooding tide maroons a field mouse on a plate-sized hummock, where it is nabbed by one of my three crows. Along with the crows, gulls and eagles linger, a monochromatic trio of winter scavengers.

The first snow is followed the next day by a heavier snowfall, and during this time the land-fast ice begins to creep out from both sides of the riverbank, two sheets moving inexorably toward each other, to shut down the river for the winter.

Finally, it seems, the heron takes the hint, and I last see it, near dusk, flying poker straight through driving snow toward the coast, its blue-gray body seeming to meld into the elements. It can only mean one thing: one morning, soon, I will wake and the river will be frozen fast.

November

12

December

THE BOY AT THE WINDOW

THERE ARE unaccountable things in nature.

I am in my study reading a passage in a story I am writing about the James Bay Cree's struggle to stave off hydropower development on their native rivers: "I am hunkered down on a salt marsh at the mouth of the Rupert River, lying in the rich tidal muds with hunters who are calling in the snow geese, wheeling around us."

As I read, I hear the geese calling back.

It takes me a moment to sort out that this is not an auditory hallucination created by the suggestion of the written word. Not quite believing my ears, I get up from my desk and go outside on the deck. At first I hear nothing, but shortly the sounds of geese reach me and I look to the southwest to see a long, wavy line of geese passing over.

What would a Cree hunter make of this? Would he believe in the magical power of his own words as incantation to call the geese into his world? But in Western culture we are not inclined to believe in such magic, such sympathetic correspondence between ourselves and nature, and pass off such events as coincidence. There is a sadness in this separation of the human and other-than-human worlds, for it drains the wonder out of an experience where spirits appear to cross paths.

SURELY THE GEESE ARE DEPARTING the strait and its river estuaries for their own reasons, but not in a linear or entirely predictable way. They fly south on northerly winds, then wheel and return to their feeding grounds when the weather moderates. They will stay as long as there is open water and they can get at the last of the green fodder that fuels their ultimate migration. Caught out by bad weather, they will seek shelter on the marshes and tuck their heads under their wings against the withering first snows.

Ice pans, too, come and go in the river, building up during brief cold snaps and retreating during thaws. At night these ghostly presences grind with an inexorable force, jamming and diving under and over one another, and sometimes jumping the riverbanks to lodge on the lower reaches of our lawn and the marsh.

I step out into a still night, two days before the full moon, its high brightness shrouded by cloud at eleven-thirty. A sound bears down on me out of this hushed hour; an ice floe—white against the black waters—rounds the bend, bearing down on me like a locomotive. It shatters the shell ice, clatters, skates like fingernails on the blackboard of the night. Light from the moon and the halogen street lamps along our country road glance off the ridges, momentarily illuminating the chaos. Then the floe passes, a dark orchestration, the sawing of a cosmic fiddle scraping toward the sea.

More than spectacle, this ice performs a vital ecological function. As it grinds and skids across the marsh, it crops last summer's grasses, sheering off the spartina at ground level. The tide carries it away to the strait, where it will begin the slow process of decay, first being broken down by bacteria and fungi, which will be ingested by higher life-forms. This marsh harvest will form a major pool of nutrients in the marine ecosystem, fueling it from bottom to top.

Freeze-up is the final act in the four-season symphony of the marsh. In the coming winter survival will become a grim matter of resistance or withdrawal into dormancy.

OUR FIRST WINTERS here I was apprehensive about how the fox and the eagle would survive the freeze-up of the river and marsh, but they do, working with the tides to find food and to cope with the ever-colder days.

In the wake of the large early winter tides, the fox appears on the marsh to scavenge, its luxuriant coat the color of the ruined grasses. It moves onto the marsh purposefully but with caution, as if trying not to get its feet wet. It assumes a hunched, intent posture, head down, its nose leading its search for food. Occasionally the fox stops and digs at the light crust of snow, using its paws and nose to lever the frozen surface and uncover some morsel the tide brought in or loosened from the marsh's hold. In time I learn that it is no coincidence that the fox should appear the day after an extreme high tide. It knows that something good to eat might have been churned up by the flood.

Other creatures also take advantage of the shifting conditions on the marsh, controlled by the cold and the tides that in December are constant antagonists, alternately forming the first ice and breaking it apart.

On my daily walk, the dog's barking alerts me to a mink across the river. A mink has hunting routes of 1.5 to 3 kilometers (1 to 2 miles), which it regularly patrols. Like the fox, it seems to do a circuit of the dyke around the Old Marsh. Long and lithe, it ripples when it runs, its supple backbone seeming to propel its forward motion. This litheness and thinness allows it to disappear into tiny holes, working its way in and out of small crevices of ice like thread through the eye of a needle—and into the winter dens of the muskrat, where the male mink makes predatory raids.

The ultimate opportunists, crows keep watch all winter. As the tide breaks up the river ice, I see marooned on one of the floes a black vulnerable speck, probably a star-nosed mole, which is semiaquatic and well adapted to marsh habitat. I happen to look out at the crucial moment, when a menacing flock of crows is hovering above the ice and its doomed stowaway. The mole rears up on its hind legs in a vain attempt to defend itself, but it is impossible. A crow plucks it neatly away by the neck and flies off over the flooding marsh with its furry meal.

Crows also dine on the sticklebacks fast-frozen by the cold nights and released the next day on the flood tide. They have competition, however. The little fish attract the attention of three bald eagles. Two are the year's young, while the other is older, sporting a nearly white head but retaining some mottling on the tail. They circle and harass the crows for the silver prizes flashing in their black beaks. The crows return as good as they get, dive-bombing the young eagles, which jockey and make menacing gestures toward each other. Even as they fly off, the eagles parry in the sky above Lucius's Marsh.

Such aggression over sticklebacks—appetizers at best—underscores the paucity of resources, which will haunt the eagles all winter.

AS LONG AS THERE IS open water, the fishers will remain, hedging their bets that they can find enough food to balance their caloric losses to the cooling air. Hoarfrost sparkles on the marsh stems, and the birches are exquisite glass trees in the early-morning hours. The nearly frozen-over river continues to breathe at the edges, however, great exhalations of vapor billowing up. The river remains open longest at the *aboiteau,* where the constant drainage from the marsh retards ice formation. Standing there stoically is a great blue heron, his white head buried deeply in his hunched shoulders.

I fret over the fate of this bird, worrying that it has stayed too late or is simply too old to make another migration. As the days count down toward Christmas, warm rains wipe clean the buildup of snow and ice; the river again opens up, issuing a reprieve.

It has always excited me merely to apprehend another living thing. I now recognize I am most like that heron—eye-hungry, ever watchful, predatory, listening. This hunting for stimuli feeds a spiritual hunger.

I have never believed in the Christian view that the birds, or the other parts of nature, were there for my edification. My fellow "biotic citizens"—to borrow the beautiful phrase coined by the great twentieth-century conservationist Aldo Leopold—have merely made my life more livable. They have brought me joy and surprise, sometimes fear, and often humility and respect. They have imparted to me a sense of place, of sharing and belonging to a larger community, one that is not exclusively human. But mostly, they have inspired wonder at the intricacies of the animate world.

On an intellectual level, I know that their presence is a sign that the ecosystem is healthy, and there is comfort in that knowledge, for their welfare and my own. But my enduring attachment to the animals and the plants is far more sensual than it is cerebral. My delight in their being is little changed from when my mother cradled me in her arms and held me up to the window to see the moonlight on the marsh, and I exclaimed, "Ducks," at seeing the dark, distinctive shapes adrift on the sequined water.

The inherent value of living things, as Leopold himself recognized, is "uncaptured by language." Regardless, this is what a nature writer tries to do, capture "the others" in a net of words. I obsessively watch the seasonal changes in the landscape—the greening and ungreening of the marsh. And the incidental changes—for example, the fall of a tree, which leaves a bright new gash on the landscape and will immediately attract the attention of a pileated woodpecker seeking insects, or the settling into the marsh bank of a piece of driftwood shaped like plow handles that will become a perch for a kingfisher. These mundane phenomena are a daily delight. They drive the incremental, geological narrative of this place. The passage of the seasons, the daily weather, are cinematic effects that entrain and focus all the senses in this grand, ongoing story.

I share this drama with the other salt marsh residents of the Old Marsh, its willets, White Birch Foxes, and sharp-tailed sparrows, and its other rare and regular visitors. I do not understand all the motives and outcomes of their actions, but merely by the act of looking, of participating in their lives at a distance, I am nourished. Ultimately, all that is important is knowing that they are there, as they, or those like them, have been since the remotest time out of memory, and that their kind might survive as long as such wetlands are preserved.

A WETLAND SEPARATED the back of our property from the Yarmouth airport runway. I am old enough to remember the frightful sound of the DC-3s returning from Boston, the propellers' turbulence shaking the house and rattling Mother's dishes in the china cabinet as the planes passed low over the farmhouse roof. By the late 1950s, however, the airline wanted to replace the outdated prop planes with jet service, which required lengthening the runway, extending it closer to our back line and the source of the farm's namesake brook.

The summer that work began on the project coincided with what at first seemed inexplicable: an oily slick appeared on the previously pristine woodland stream. As summer wore on, an orangish scum accumulated on the rocks, a grotesque algal bloom that made the water so foul smelling and uninviting that my mother gave up going to the swimming hole and I no longer played at the brook mouth because of the noxious pollution. Everything pointed to the work being done on the runway as the source. It was a sad end to what would prove to be my last summer on the farm and the marsh. It was also an event that would have a profound influence on my future, steering me in the direction of environmentalism, a movement that had yet to be officially born.

My grandmother died the winter we moved to town. Daily my mother kept vigil at the nursing home and returned home, exhausted, to a sick child. All the while I was recovering from my own illness, brooding about returning to the farm, and by mid-April I was well enough to bike the 8 kilometers (5 miles), balancing my fishing rod across my handlebars and a lunch upon my back like the vagabond in the popular school chorale. It seems I had forgotten about the poisonous effluent in the brook, imagining it still unsullied and beckoning as always to the little, crimson-bellied sea trout that every spring ran in from the salt water to deposit their packets of milt and spawn in the woodland pools above the tide.

I biked the New Road to the railway tracks and began by fishing the pools on the meadow, places where in summer big trout often lay. Finding none, I battled through thickets of alders, dabbling in the small pools along the way until I reached a deep pool where a jagged, moss-covered outcrop spilled its waters. As I always did, I sat on the root of a yellow birch, which formed a ready-made seat where it clung to the bank. The water now seemed clean, as did the rocks, having been scoured no doubt by the spring runoff—but there were no fish. I was still optimistic, thinking perhaps the fish had not yet migrated to the upper reaches of the brook. I worked my way down to a broad, shallow pool in the shadow of a high bank and began to drift my worm in the current. It was then I noticed something in the water: a trout, belly-up, floating around and around in a back eddy, its bright body already clouded by fungus. It was the only trout I saw that day, and it was the last time I returned to fish on Brook Farm.

I biked back to town, empty-handed and brokenhearted. The stark image of the dead trout eddied in my consciousness for decades.

Several years ago, I returned to Brook Farm, driving to the end of New Road, now renamed Lewis Road for the former occupants of my childhood home. I wanted to confirm whether what I had always believed was true: that the runoff from the airport runway had ruined the brook. I parked the car where the road ended, at the rail bed for the old Dominion Atlantic

Railroad, which once linked the communities along the South Shore of Nova Scotia but decades ago had been abandoned. I walked along the rail bed; the tracks and ties, which I had straddled and jumped as a boy, had been torn up. The brook paralleled the rail bed and, several hundred meters along, passed under it, though the small rail bridge was now gone. I stopped and looked into the water. It was summer and the water moved slowly, but I could see a heavy load of sediment filtering through it. There was no sign of trout. I walked back to the road, from where I could see the airport runway rising above the wetland that was the source of the brook. There was now no doubt in my mind that the runoff from the airport had been, and still was, the cause of the death of the brook.

I drove back to the main road and parked at the bottom of the lane that led to the old farmhouse, now painted and standing proudly atop the hill. I walked across the field toward the salt marsh, following an imaginary path that I had once taken to the mouth of the brook, where so long ago I had fished for eels and smelt. I moved through the green sward of the spartina to the creek. The swimming hole had filled in with sediment, deposited by the brook on its way to the sea. The marsh spread out before me, however, as verdant and vital as it had always seemed. Far off, I heard the cry of a willet; in the silence that followed, I also heard the faint song of the sharp-tailed sparrow secreted somewhere in the grasses. The brook had died (for what is a brook without fish) and, with it, my then-naïve trust in society's will to preserve habitat in the name of progress. But the salt marsh was, for now, still a living place, still home to the birds of my boyhood, still a place of wonder.

IN 1980 CATHY and I purchased a run-down Acadian-style home, or *habitant,* which had been built in the 1820s and at one time in its checkered history had served as a sheep barn. At the end of a cul-de-sac, it perched halfway up one of the eroded mountains of the Appalachian chain that cut across northern Nova Scotia. Besides the 1½-story post-and-beam house, there was a large derelict barn, a chicken house, and a small garage. This abandoned farmstead occupied 12 hectares (30 acres), more or less, of sour hay fields, blueberry land, and a wooded ravine through which ran the West Brook. For me it satisfied a twenty-year longing to return to "the farm." Although it was only a halfway measure of really going back to the land, as many of our generation had done, we tended large kitchen gardens, raised chickens for meat and eggs, and, in spring, tapped the old ornamental sugar maples for their sweet sap. Also in spring I fished with Meg for trout along the rills and pools of the little brook as I had as a child on Brook Farm. In the fall, salmon re-turned from the sea to seek their ancestral spawning redds. The only thing missing in this nostalgic tapestry of landscape was the salt marsh.

When our daughter was still young and we were living in the 180-year-old farmstead, we woke one Christmas morning to a heavy snowfall—great, thick flakes that formed a perforated blind through which it was barely possible to discern the land-scape. It would block the road, and this being a holiday, the plow would not arrive until midnight, breaking through the banks like Strelnikov's train in *Doctor Zhivago,* pushing great white rooster tails of snow into the ditches. We reveled in the prospect of being briefly cut off from the world, a loving family adrift in time.

Our dining room table looked out on an old apple orchard in the backyard. We rose early to greet Meg's excitement at what Santa had brought her. But we were met by another kind of sur-prise. Standing in the orchard, pawing at the ground for frozen fruit, was a great buck, its luxurious tawny coat catching and accumulating a layer of snow that clung to it like cotton batting. This old, wily animal—its antlers sported fourteen points for each one of its years on Earth—had come down from the mountain under the cover of the storm, drawn into the dangerous, to him, sphere of humans by the fermenting fruit. They must have tasted good, for he ate slowly, apparently oblivious to us as we sat entranced at the dining room table, mere meters away.

Finally, the buck had eaten enough and moved back to his mountain domain, carving a deep trail through the growing banks of snow. It felt as if the spirit of the land, as the Cree goose hunter had told me, had recognized us.

When I was growing up on Brook Farm, domestic animals, those of the Nativity, were integral to the magic of Christmas. I believed in reindeer, of course, particularly because of the words of the then-current, now-classic, song by Gene Autry, "Rudolf the Red-Nosed Reindeer." The lyrics seemed to be penned with the climate I knew in mind: Christmases were often foggy at the southern tip of Nova Scotia, where the average winter temperature hovers around the freezing point and snow rarely stays on the ground for long. Herons and waterfowl—perhaps the same ones I see here in late fall—may feed there all winter. Fog often spoiled the classic picture of Christmas, of country houses and barns swathed in Currier-and-Ives snowbanks, but I knew that Rudolf, "with his nose so bright," would come through the fog that was our soggy, winter blanket.

Our ritual on Christmas morning was to open our stockings at breakfast, but we had to wait until Dad returned from milking the cows and had his own breakfast to gather around the tree for presents. This delayed gratification required an extraordinary act of will. The parlor where the tree was ensconced in a bay window was at the foot of the stairs. I had to avert my eyes as I passed the doorway in order not to catch an inadvertent glance of Santa's gifts under the tree. I learned to do this, knowing it prolonged the deliciousness of the day.

The mythology of Christmas, with its mangers and cattle lowing, seemed invented to suit my bucolic circumstances. Even now, though I have no cows to milk, our family keeps the tradition of only opening presents after breakfast and then only one at a time to make the day last.

MY MOTHER USED TO SAY, "Little ducks quack before walking through a puddle." What she meant by this homily was to beware of what we say because we might find ourselves, in life's unexpected twists and turns, doing the very things we once protested. So in 1990, after ten years of what I jokingly refer to as "splendid isolation," Cathy and I decided to leave the farm. As my parents had done, much to my childhood grief, we thought a move closer to town would be better both for Meg, then eight, and for Cathy, who would be closer to her workplace.

It was a difficult decision, not only because we had been happy on the farm but because we were abandoning the land for a postage-stamp building lot and a modern split-level home that had none of the charm of our renovated farmhouse, with its wide pine boards and rough-hewn beams. But on one side of the road, we were gaining neighbors who were longtime friends and had children the same age as our daughter. And across the Tidnish River was the Old Marsh. In midlife, after a circuitous journey, I had found my way back to the environment of my childhood.

Visits from wild animals to the Old Marsh have limned Christmases of the recent past. They are a kind of blessing.

In our new home, two days before Christmas, we hear an owl, plaintively calling near midnight: *ho-hoo, hoo, hoo, hoo.* It is close by, and we open the living room door, despite the cold, so Cathy and I can hear it better. Frost billows into the living room, as does the haunting call that seems to be coming from the tree line on our side of the river.

It is a great horned owl, and two days later, it is still keeping company with us. At midnight on Christmas Day, I startle the great bird from its roost on the breezeway roof. I hear its talons scrape against the grit of the asphalt shingles as it makes purchase and takes flight, but it glides away soundlessly on those silent wings.

I wonder what attracts this night hunter to our door, what affinities we share.

IT IS CHRISTMAS AGAIN, only this year it is green, like so many Christmases of my childhood. The marsh and the river are completely open, even at this late date. As I hand out the presents from under the tree, one by one, I notice an odd V-shaped disturbance in the water, but in my excitement I ignore it for the moment, thinking it might be nothing more than a contrary movement of water in the wind.

I take a break from playing Father Christmas and go down to the basement to check on the wood fire, when I hear Meg calling, "Dad, there's a seal in the river!" I run upstairs in time to see a harbor seal, its silver-gray coat decorated with abstract black splotches, turn and take an impressively long dive, creating a wake like the one I had ignored before.

Head up, he chugs downriver. We watch in silence as he disappears.

NOTES

Notes refer to direct quotations. Numbers at left refer to pages where the quotations occur.

16–17   David Abram, *The Spell of the Sensuous: Perception and Language in a More-than-human World* (New York: Pantheon Books, 1996), pp. 49, 52.

35   H.G.C. Ketchum, "The Chignecto Ship Railway," in *The World's Columbian Water Commerce Congress* (Boston: Damrell & Upham, 1893), pp. 3–12.

41   Henry David Thoreau, "Notes on New England birds" (1910), as quoted in Arthur Cleveland Bent, *Life Histories of North American Cardinals, Grosbeaks, Buntings, Towhees, Finches, Sparrows and Allies: Part One* (New York: Dover Publications, 1968), p. 408.

43   Tomas Tranströmer, "From March '79," in *Selected Poems, 1954–1986,* translated by Robert Bly et al., edited by Robert Hass (New York: Ecco Press, 1987).

49   Henry David Thoreau, *Walden and Civil Disobedience* (1855), edited by
      Sherman Paul (Cambridge, Mass.: Riverside Cambridge Press, 1960),
      p. 206.

67   Thoreau, *Walden and Civil Disobedience,* p. 206.

69   Harry Thurston, "Wood Duck," from "Arcadia: The Marsh Suite" in
      If Men Lived On Earth (Kentville, N.S.: Gaspereau Press, 2000), p. 66.

70   Charles Darwin, *The Descent of Man and Selection in Relation to Sex*
      (1871), as quoted by Adrian Forsyth, *The Nature of Birds* (Camden East,
      Ont.: Camden House Publishing, 1988), p. 29.

70   Edward O. Wilson, *Consilience: The Unity of Knowledge* (New York: Alfred
      A. Knopf, 1998), pp. 231–32.

100   Gary Kowalski, *The Souls of Animals* (Walpole, N.H.: Stillpoint Publish-
      ing, 1991), pp. 85–92.

106   Gerard Manley Hopkins, "As kingfishers catch fire, dragonflies
      draw flame," in *Poems and Prose of Gerard Manley Hopkins,* edited by
      W.H. Gardner (Harmondsworth: Penguin Books, 1972), p. 51.

121   Robie W. Tufts, *The Birds of Nova Scotia* (Halifax: Nova Scotia Museum,
      1973), p. 199.

121–23 Harrison F. Lewis, "The Willet (*Catoptrophorus semipalmatus
        semipalmatus*) in Nova Scotia," *The Auk* 37 (1920): 581–82.

124–25 Harrison F. Lewis, "Notes on the Acadian Sharp-tailed Sparrow (*Passer-
        herbulus nelsoni subvirgatus*)," *The Auk* 37 (1920): 587–89.

135   John and Mildred Teal, *The Life and Death of the Salt Marsh* (New York:
      Ballantine Books, 1983), p. 84.

136   Carl Linnaeus, *Praeludia Sponsaliorum Plantarum* (1729), as quoted by
      Londa Schiebinger, "The Loves of the Plants," *Scientific American* 274
      (February 1996): 110–15.

141–42 J.W. Dawson, "On a Modern Submerged Forest at Fort Lawrence,
        Nova Scotia," *Quarterly Journal, London Geological Society* 11 (1855):
        119–22.

144 Fred A. Hatfield, "Man Comes Forward to Say He Knows What Happened to Missing Boy," *The Yarmouth Vanguard* 29 (February 24, 1995): 1–2.

150–51 Charles Kingsley, *The Water Babies* (1863; reprint, New York: dilithium Press, Ltd., Children's Classics Division, 1986), pp. 47–48.

163 Harrison F. Lewis, "Eelgrass and Other Waterfowl Food: Present Status and Future Prospects," in *Wildlife Restoration and Conservation: Proceedings of the North American Wildlife Conference* (Washington, D.C.: United States Government Printing Office, 1936), pp. 91–92.

172 Alan Ruffman, "A Multi-disciplinary and Inter-scientific Study of the Saxby Gale: An October 4–5, 1869 hybrid hurricane and record storm surge," *CMOS Bulletin* 27 (1999): 67–73. Source: http://is.dal.ca/~es/seminars/1999/1999-sem-ar.htm.

179–80 Stuart Tingley and Wayne Barrett, *Wings Over Water: Water Birds of the Atlantic* (Halifax: Nimbus Publishing, 1991), p. 21.

196 Harvey Feit, "Hunting and the Quest for Power: The James Bay Cree and Whitemen in the Twentieth Century," in *Native Peoples: The Canadian Experience,* edited by R. Bruce Morrison and C. Roderick Wilson (Toronto: McClelland and Stewart, 1986), pp. 171–207.

199–200 Carl G. Jung et al., *Man and His Symbols* (Garden City, N.Y.: Doubleday & Company, 1964), p. 52.

200 Hugh Brody, *Maps and Dreams* (New York: Pantheon Books, 1981), p. 44.

200 Thoreau, *Walden and Civil Disobedience,* p. 89.

213 Lewis J. Poteet, *The South Shore Phrase Book: A Nova Scotia Dictionary* (Hantsport, N.S.: Lancelot Press, 1983), p. 22.

214 Annie Dillard, *An American Childhood* (New York: Harper & Row, Publishers, 1987), p. 3.